Problems in Philosophy

Problems in Philosophy

The Limits of Inquiry

Colin McGinn

BLACKWELL
Oxford UK & Cambridge USA

Copyright © Colin McGinn 1993

The right of Colin McGinn to be identified as author of this work has been asserted in accordance with the Copyright, Designs and Patents Act 1988.

First published 1993

Blackwell Publishers
108 Cowley Road
Oxford OX4 1JF
UK

238 Main Street
Cambridge, Massachusetts 02142
USA

British Library Cataloguing in Publication Data

A CIP catalogue record for this book is available from the British Library.

Library of Congress Cataloging-in-Publication Data

McGinn, Colin, 1950–
    Problems in philosophy : the limits of inquiry / Colin McGinn.
      p. cm.
    ISBN 1–55786–474–8 (alk. paper). — ISBN 1–55786–475–6 (pbk. : alk. paper)
    1. Knowledge, Theory of. 2. Philosophy of mind. 3. Philosophy.
I. Title.
    BD161.M385 1993
    101—dc20
                                                          93–14752
                                                              CIP

Typeset in 11 on 13 pt Sabon
by Graphicraft Typesetters Ltd., Hong Kong
Printed in Great Britain

This book is printed on acid-free paper

Contents

Preface

I suspect that many people are attracted to philosophy precisely because its questions appear so hard to answer. No obvious method for answering these questions suggests itself, yet they seem peculiarly profound and interesting. Philosophical knowledge would thus be uniquely deep and satisfying, and we are under a special obligation to pursue it. There is even a certain nobility attached to grappling with these questions, as if we are dealing with an exceptionally elevated region of reality. The hardness of philosophy is part of its charm.

This book offers an account of the nature of philosophical difficulty, an account which can only be described as deflationary. According to this account, the hardness of philosophy is both subjective and irremediable. I do not anticipate an enthusiastic reception for this view. I myself came round to it only slowly and reluctantly. Some years ago I became convinced that the mind–body problem is insoluble by the human intellect, despite its being objectively undistinguished among questions about nature; but at that time I did not believe that the same kind of diagnosis applied to other philosophical questions. Subsequent reflection, however, led me to conclude, after some vacillation, that this type of view is more widely applicable than seemed so at first sight. The present book gives the reasons why I came to think this.

The following people made helpful comments along the way: Malcolm Budd, Jerry Fodor, Tony Mesa, Jonathan Miller, Thomas Nagel, Consuelo Preti, Galen Strawson. At a graduate seminar I gave at Princeton I enjoyed the sympathetic criticism of, among others, Alex Burn, Fiona Cowie and David Sosa. My greatest debt is to Noam Chomsky – for the stimulus provided by his work, for much encouraging and probing correspondence, and for detailed comments on the penultimate draft of the book. I would also like to thank my department at Rutgers for giving me leave and for the wholesome intellectual atmosphere there.

Colin McGinn
New York

1
Philosophical Perplexity

I Transcendental Naturalism

Philosophical theses can sometimes be assented to, but often they can expect only to be taken seriously. We may hope to find sufficient reason actually to believe a philosophical proposition, but often enough the best we can do is get ourselves into a position to regard the proposition with respect. We rate it a contender. The set of such propositions constitutes the range of options we think *may* be true: they cannot be ruled out and there are considerations that speak in their favour. We might, on occasion, have reasons – more or less indirect, or large-scale – that make us suspect that a certain hypothesis *must* be true, without being able to show *how* this is so. The hypothesis may not engage our beliefs in the simple way other hypotheses do, in science or common sense, yet we find ourselves irresistibly drawn to it: something like this, we feel, *has* to be so, if only because it is preferable to its rivals. A good deal of philosophical debate consists in persuading others to take seriously a hypothesis one has come to find attractive for reasons that defy summary statement or straightforward demonstration; one tries to exhibit the virtues of the hypothesis, especially as compared to the available alternatives. Or, failing even that, one argues that the hypothesis cannot be excluded. One limits oneself, modestly, to soliciting philosophical respect, recognizing that philosophical belief is too much to expect – not to speak of philosophical certainty. And this shows something significant about the nature of philosophy – about the epistemology of philosophical inquiry. The relation between evidence (argument) and truth is very often not close enough to permit full-blown assent. Hence the magnitude and intractability of much philosophical disagreement.

My aim in this book is to try out a very general hypothesis. The attitude I intend to produce towards the hypothesis is mere respect; if the reader ends up believing it, that is his or her own business. In the nature of the case, indeed, it is a hypothesis which does not admit of the kind of demonstration we naturally demand for hypotheses of its general form. My claim will be that the hypothesis may be true, and that much would make sense if it were. I shall proceed as follows. In this chapter I shall set out, in a preliminary way, what the hypothesis says, explain the conception of philosophical problems it entails, and sketch the geography of philosophical debate it predicts. This will serve to introduce the basic perspective and the conceptual apparatus needed to articulate it. In the next six chapters I shall apply the hypothesis to a number of specific issues, treating the problem of consciousness as a philosophical paradigm, testing the plausibility of the hypothesis and drawing out its consequences: here is where I hope to sow the seeds of philosophical respect. Chapter 8 will draw this material together and explore the claims of human reason to be the route to philosophical truth. The following chapter will briefly compare the resulting view of philosophy with some other views, arguing for its superiority. Throughout we shall be operating at a high altitude, covering a lot of ground in a rather abstract and tendentious fashion, stressing metaphilosophical themes. The discussion will often be distressingly speculative and schematic, even by philosophical standards.

What, then, is this putatively reputable hypothesis? Very simply it can be put as follows: philosophical perplexities arise in us because of definite inherent limitations on our epistemic faculties, not because philosophical questions concern entities or facts that are intrinsically problematic or peculiar or dubious. Philosophy is an attempt to get outside the constitutive structure of our minds. Reality itself is everywhere flatly natural, but because of our cognitive limits we are unable to make good on this general ontological principle. Our epistemic architecture obstructs knowledge of the real nature of the objective world. I shall call this thesis *transcendental naturalism*, TN for short. Let us now try to sharpen TN up a bit, explaining its motivation and key concepts, preferably without the aid of metaphor.

We need, first, to make some basic distinctions among questions that may interest the enquiring mind. Four sorts of question may confront a particular type of cognitive being B: problems, mysteries, illusions, issues.[1] A *problem* is a question to which B can in principle find the answer, and is perhaps designed so to do, for biological or other reasons; or at least is of such a *type* as B can answer. Everyday life and much of science consists of solving problems – questions that fall within our cognitive bounds. A *mystery* is a question that does not differ from a problem in point of the naturalness of its subject-matter, but only in respect of the contingent cognitive capacities that B possesses: the mystery is a mystery *for that being*. An *illusion* is (or arises from) some kind of pseudo-question, or a question that is so formulated as to suggest an answer of a kind that does not objectively exist. An illusory question is not to be confused with a mysterious one, which latter reflects ill on B, not on the question. An *issue* is a question, typically of a normative character, about which B creatures may dispute, and with respect to which no scientific theory is suited as an answer – questions of ethics and politics, say.

Note, what is vital, that the categories of problem and mystery are defined in a relative way – the division turns upon the specific cognitive make-up of the class of thinking creatures we are considering.[2] In principle, two sorts of creature might invert each other's characteristic division of questions into problems and mysteries, depending on their epistemic talents and endowments. Indeed, the mystery class for one sort of creature might be *innately* soluble by the other, and this be manifested at an early age too. Let us say that such creatures differ in the 'cognitive space' through which their minds can move, rather as there exist species-specific differences in the motor spaces through which creatures can physically move, given their natural constitution (birds and fish, say). Then the idea of a mystery is simply the idea of a question that happens to fall outside a given creature's cognitive space. It is analogous to the idea of items that lie outside of a creature's phenomenal or perceptual or affective space – sensations it cannot feel, properties it cannot perceive, emotions it cannot experience. If we suppose that creatures possess 'organs' that define these spaces, then mysteries are questions for which the given creature lacks the requisite intellectual organ(s).[3] The totality of these spaces would constitute the mental horizon of the type of creature in question.

We can also capture the underlying idea here by means of a counterfactual about a given creature: take a question that is a mere problem for the creature (say, a human being) and imagine the creature to have the relevant problem-solving capacities removed, so that the question is no longer answerable by that creature. In the counterfactual case, then, there is no intrinsic change in the ontological status of the topic of the question – we have simply moved to a situation in which the relevant creature now lacks the epistemic capacities to comprehend that topic. By hypothesis, the change is purely epistemic. Steam engines do not turn occult when the possible world in which they exist happens to lack any creatures with the mental capacity to understand their workings. And the converse shift, from mystery to problem, likewise involves no sudden access of ontological purity. This is really no more than to insist on the epistemic character of the distinction.

According to TN about a certain question Q with respect to a being B, the subject-matter of Q has three properties: (i) reality, (ii) naturalness, and (iii) epistemic inaccessibility to B. Q does not harbour an illusion (hence (i)), nor does it refer to entities or properties that are intrinsically non-natural (hence (ii)), yet the answer to Q is beyond the capacities of B creatures (hence (iii)). Thus TN contrasts, not only with illusion theses about Q, but also with three other positions, as follows. Immanent naturalism takes all genuine questions to have answers in the space of theories accessible to B, and it is comprehensively naturalistic. Immanent non-naturalism accepts an ontological bifurcation into the natural and the non-natural but insists on the comprehensibility to B of both sides of the bifurcation, perhaps in virtue of supernatural capacities on the part of B. Transcendent non-naturalism asserts that some questions invoke facts that are both supernatural and beyond the capacity of B to comprehend. TN, for its part, makes no ontological division into the natural and the non-natural, but it is happy with an epistemological division into the answerable and the unanswerable. In fact, it is truer to the intentions of TN to avoid any positive use of the term 'natural', since this implies a well-defined distinction between the natural and the non-natural; better to think of TN as opposing the very idea of the non- or super-natural altogether. TN is anti-non-naturalistic: it is the negative thesis that there is no sense to be made of the ontological category of the non-natural. It regards such notions as distorted reflections of epistemic quandaries, not as signifying meaningful objective categories.[4] (This should become clearer later when we see TN in operation.)

Plainly TN accepts a strong form of realism; in particular, it accepts realism about the *nature* of the things that cognitive beings think and talk about. While we may be able to refer to certain things, there is no guarantee that we shall be able to develop adequate theories of these things. Put differently, the correct theory of what is referred to, conceived as a set of propositions detailing the nature of those referents, may not belong in the space of theories accessible to the beings under consideration – including human thinkers. So, for TN, there may exist facts about the world that are inaccessible to thinking creatures such as ourselves. Reality is under no epistemic constraint.[5]

TN, as I am defining it, incorporates a double naturalism (or anti-non-naturalism – I shall drop this periphrasis from now on): both about reality and about our knowledge of it. The natural world can transcend our knowledge of it precisely because our knowledge is a natural fact about us, in relation to that world. It is a general property of evolved organisms, such as ourselves, to exhibit areas of cognitive weakness or incapacity, resulting from our biological constitution; so it is entirely reasonable to expect naturally based limits to human understanding. We are not gods, cognitively speaking. A creature's mental powers are things *in* the natural world, with a natural origin, function and structure, and there is no necessity that this part of the world should be capable of taking in the rest. The 'transcendent' component of TN simply gives expression to this naturalism about the mind.

The transcendence envisaged by TN can take stronger or weaker forms, and many versions of it can be formulated. For my purposes, the most pertinent distinction to introduce is between *bias* theses and *closure* theses. A bias thesis holds that the faculties of B are skewed away from certain questions, possibly because they are skewed towards others. More precisely, and adopting a modular conception of cognitive capacity, we think of B's epistemic potential as the sum of its several cognitive modules – special-purpose domain-specific systems – and these modules will have inbuilt principles biasing them away from dealing with certain types of question. For example, the human language module is negatively biased with respect to certain definable languages, and it is no use at all in developing other sorts of knowledge.[6] Within a given type of creature the bias of a module M1 may be compensated for by a distinct module M2, so that the creature is able in principle to know what M1 prohibits – as we might laboriously learn languages for which our given language module is unsuited by exploiting our general capacity for theory construction. But it is also possible that the biases of the totality of the creature's modules completely rule out acquiring certain sorts of knowledge. In the former kind of case the creature will experience considerable subjective difficulty in acquiring the knowledge in question, no matter what objective properties the domain in question possesses. In the latter kind of case there will be no escape from the cognitive bias and ignorance will be irremediable: the bias will lead to closure. If we picture the mind as analogous to a Swiss army knife, where each gadget corresponds to a cognitive faculty, then there will be tasks for which no gadget on the model of knife in question can do the job and tasks for which a gadget designed for one kind of job can be pressed into service in executing another. Given the truth of a negative bias thesis with respect to a certain subject-matter, of either of these two kinds, we would expect all the symptoms of immense difficulty, both behavioural and subjective, combined with no special reason to suppose that we have entered the realm of the inherently inscrutable or impossibly complex. And this may alter our conception of the nature of that subject-matter. Bias does not, then, entail closure, though it may well underlie it in cases for which closure holds. Neither does closure entail bias – or not obviously. A question may be necessarily unanswerable for a creature consistently with a *tabula rasa* conception of that creature's mind: that is, we can view cognitive capacity as non-modular and undifferentiated, as a 'general-purpose learning machine', and still hold that certain questions exceed the limits of such a mind, say by dint of sheer complexity.[7] Bias theses entail a particular view of cognitive structure; closure theses imply merely the existence of cognitive limits.

Now if our class of questions is that of philosophy, we can formulate TN either in terms of closure or bias, or closure in virtue of bias. A bias thesis by itself is weaker than a closure thesis in that it allows the possibility of solving philosophical problems; what it claims, however, is that there is a mismatch between module and question in the philosophical case. Hence the difficulty of arriving at philosophical knowledge: the epistemic characteristics of philosophical questions result from a systematic bias away from the subject-matter of those questions. In what follows much of the discussion will be neutral between these two interpretations of TN, though it will become apparent that I am inclined towards a thesis of modular closure.

A fanciful parable may help to bring out the import of TN for the nature of philosophical questions. Imagine a race of intelligent beings who suffer from the following cognitive deficit: they can form no conception of what it would be for material objects to have atomic structure – in particular, for objects to contain internal spatial interstices. They cannot help but think of objects as having a continuous structure, with no empty space inside them. They understand the idea of gaps between macroscopic objects, but a quirk of their conceptual system prevents them forming even so much as the idea of gaps within objects. Now suppose these thinkers ask themselves, as well they might, how it is possible to divide an object into parts, or how an object can be compressed. And let us assume, for the sake of argument, that these questions have a unique solution in atomic theory: objects are divisible or compressible in virtue of the gaps that separate their smaller parts. Then, given all this, we can say that these questions are unanswerable by the continuous-thinkers – though answerable by atomic-thinkers such as ourselves. In the sense explained earlier, these questions belong in the class of mysteries for them, because they have a bias in favour of continuity that generates closure with respect to questions whose answers require knowledge of (simple) atomic theory.

Similar examples could be given by imagining creatures who cannot form concepts of three-dimensional space, or who cannot form the concept of a negative number, or whose notion of causality is limited to mental causation, or who can only think about the present, and so forth. In all these cases we can envisage questions that require conceptual and theoretical resources that exceed the contingent limits of the creatures in question. And the TN hypothesis would (virtually by stipulation) be true of them. Specifically, their mysteries would have the appearance of deep philosophical conundrums, analogous to our own philosophical puzzlement – that, at any rate, is what TN about human philosophy is in the business of claiming. *We* can see that the division problem, say, is just a problem in low-level science, not something that calls into question the entire ontology of material objects or requires the postulation of miracles or inexplicable brute facts. The special hardness they find in the problem is a reflection of a definite lack on their part, with no ontological implications. This is what TN says is the case with respect to the philosophical problems that trouble us. TN locates philosophical profundity in the specific cognitive deficits we suffer.[8]

II The Nature of Philosophy

Let us remind ourselves of how philosophical perplexities typically arise, and of the form they are apt to take. Common sense commits itself to various assertions about the world, including the mind. We acquire these ordinary beliefs at an early age and we take them for granted in everyday life; they probably have an innate basis and belong to a specialized component of our cognitive equipment. Then, because we are also self-reflective creatures, we turn back on our commonsense assumptions and find them to be more puzzling and problematic than we had bargained for. The concepts we habitually employ raise the kinds of disturbing questions we call 'philosophical'. A characteristic expression of this puzzlement asks how what we had hitherto taken for granted is actually so much as *possible*. Let C be a concept that provokes this kind of question: then the philosophy of C will concern itself with whether C-truths, commonly taken for granted, are, in the light of certain considerations, really capable of being true at all, and if so in what their truth might consist. C-propositions seemed to work perfectly well in practical contexts but, upon examination, they present *prima facie* impossibilities. The putative C-truths clash (it appears) with certain other beliefs we hold about the world, and the question is how to retain both or decide what to give up. We thus strive to understand the nature of C-facts in such a way that it becomes clear that the world can contain such facts. The simplest form of philosophical perplexity is accordingly expressed by the question 'What *is* X?'. Not that every philosophical question assumes this form; nor that philosophy is exclusively concerned with how-possible questions: but a substantial core of it traces back to this kind of perplexity (as we shall see in detail in later chapters). And it is a perplexity of a peculiarly knotty kind, generating intimations of ultimate mystery, a dazed sensation where knowledge ought to be.

A notable feature of these philosophical problems is that they seem to be about things in the world and yet are not answerable by empirically investigating those worldly things: that, at least, is how they naively present themselves. So they are like scientific questions in one way but unlike them in another (of course science itself may also raise philosophical questions). This can seem puzzling: if they are about worldly phenomena, why won't they yield to world-oriented investigation? Indeed, this combination of characteristics has seemed so puzzling to many (most) philosophers that they have revised the initial appearances: either the questions are not about the world after all or they really are answerable empirically. Thus we have the two dominant metaphilosophies – two conceptions of the proper subject-matter of philosophy, of the type of truth it endeavours to discover, of the right method to follow in discovering this truth. In effect, the two metaphilosophies differ in respect of the kinds of human faculty they take to be appropriate in arriving at philosophical knowledge, and hence in where we should look for philosophical enlightenment.

The two approaches are, familiarly enough: (a) the view that philosophical questions are (ultimately) empirical or scientific and (b) the view that they are (upon reflection) analytic or conceptual. The former view takes philosophy to be continuous with extant science, so that its questions become incorporated into science in the fullness of time (or else they are declared meaningless). Accordingly, the human faculties to use in doing philosophy are the same as those we use in empirical science: our powers of perceptual observation and our talent for empirically controlled theory construction. Philosophy is just the outer edge of empirical inquiry. In opposition to this we have the school, dominant for most of the present century, that radically distinguishes philosophy from science. This school regards philosophical inquiry as conceptual in topic and method: we are to answer our how-possible questions by elucidating the concepts that occur in our C-truths, using our faculty of self-reflection; or again, we must ruminate on the language we bring to bear on the sector of thought at issue. Hence the conception of philosophy that prompts what is sometimes called 'analytic philosophy' – a belief in the problem-solving potential of our ordinary concepts, once they are scrutinized aright. Philosophical knowledge will thus issue from the same human faculty that enables us to know (e.g.) that bachelors are unmarried males. This view embodies a principled optimism about the capacity of our present conceptual scheme to resolve questions about its own presuppositions; it is conceptually conservative in a way the contrasting empirical conception is not. The nature of the facts that trouble us is implicit in our ordinary C-propositions, waiting to be excavated a priori; so really the questions are about the concepts themselves, at least in the sense that we need not look beyond them.[9]

Where does TN stand in relation to these two standard positions? I shall answer this now in a sketchy and preliminary way, not intended as a defence or full account, but rather to set up the issues for later discussion. First, TN accepts at face-value that philosophical questions are about the world but are not soluble empirically: they concern the real objective nature of concept-independent phenomena, but we cannot answer them by means of empirical enquiry into those phenomena. So TN differs from the other two views while sharing an aspect of each. It accepts, with the empirical view, that philosophy is ontologically continuous with science, but it denies that this corresponds to any epistemic continuity, since we are not cognitively equipped to solve philosophical problems. On the other hand, it agrees with the analytic view in rejecting the idea that philosophical puzzlement will yield to empirical enquiry, but it denies that this is because concepts are our real concern. From TN's point of view, these rival metaphilosophies distortedly reflect the true epistemological predicament we are in: namely, that we can formulate questions about the world that we lack the faculties to answer. Understandably, then, we deny that they are about the world or insist that future science holds the key, unimaginable as this may seem. TN is pessimistic about the power of human empirical enquiry to solve philosophical problems, not because these problems involve an ontological shift from the world to our representations of it, but rather because we lack the means to reveal the objective nature of the things we refer to. Revising the philosophical appearances, as the other two views do, stems, for TN, from a reluctance to acknowledge our cognitive limits – from a kind of reflex optimism about human knowledge.

By implication, TN casts a sceptical eye on certain paradigms for philosophical enquiry that have been historically influential. Once a certain method of enquiry achieves notable results in other domains, while philosophy appears embarrassingly enmired, it is natural to hope that the way forward consists in following that method in the case of philosophy. Thus the remarkable scientific advances begun in the seventeenth century might well suggest to the hopeful enquirer that philosophical questions will succumb to essentially the same methods – or else reveal themselves not to be genuine questions at all. But TN reminds us that these methods might have a strictly defined sphere of potential success. Natural science is a product of the human mind, with its inbuilt principles and limits, and there is no good reason to believe that every question about Nature can be answered by a mind so structured and employed. Philosophy, in particular, might require styles of thought and methods of enquiry that lie outside the bounds of our capacity for empirical science. And, of course, on the face of it philosophical problems are not soluble by scientific methods. TN provides a perspective from which this epistemic discontinuity becomes intelligible.

A different paradigm, going further back, has been supplied by the formal sciences. Here I mean to include rational ethics as well as logic and mathematics – the non-empirical areas of human knowledge. The natural thought here is that philosophy should be assimilated to these subjects, on account of its non-empirical character. So we have the idea that the methods of philosophy include dialogue and argument, thesis and counter-example, proof and intuition, analysis and axiomatization. But TN questions whether the human faculties employed in those activities are appropriate for philosophy, since it cannot simply be assumed that they are, in view of the inappropriateness of empirical methods. And how is this paradigm to be squared with the apparent fact that so much of philosophy is concerned with natural phenomena, not abstract or formal matters? TN warns that such paradigms be approached with extreme caution; certainly we should not cling to them simply because no other set of methods suggests itself – for there may *be* no other method available to us. A being who could answer our philosophical questions with comparative ease might use methods and faculties that are radically disjoint from any that we possess; they may even be inconceivable by us, even in rough outline. In short, we should examine putative paradigms for philosophical knowledge on their merits and not be credulously seduced by the lack of anything better – since TN is not to be ruled out. I myself would say that the plain incredibility of the standard proposals for an epistemology of philosophy ought to make us view the TN hypothesis with some seriousness.

Any account of the epistemology of philosophy ought to have something to say about the chronic lack of progress that seems endemic to the subject, compared to other intellectual pursuits. And metaphilosophies can be evaluated according to their ability to explain this lack of steady advance. Again, without taking up the question in detail, let me just state where TN stands as compared with other views. The two standard conceptions encounter obvious *prima facie* difficulties over this question. The empirical view cannot point to the kinds of scientific advance enjoyed by its preferred paradigms: philosophy does not look much like flourishing science. There ought to be more advance than there is, under this view. The analytic view must face the question of why our concepts are so opaque and inaccessible to us: if all we have to do is spell out what our ordinary notions involve, why has it proved so hard to push the subject forward

– it ought to be easy! So, again, there should be more advance than we observe. In response to these challenges adherents offer extenuating explanations. Perhaps there is more progress than there seems, since science keeps slicing off parts of philosophy, leaving a standing residue of not-yet-solved questions.[10] Perhaps our efforts to articulate the content of our concepts are thwarted by certain temptations, misleading analogies, linguistic bewitchments, and so forth. Yet other views hold that the questions of philosophy are meaningless and hence trivially unanswerable, or that they concern matters of such intrinsic subtlety and profundity that lack of progress is hardly surprising. TN has a simple and straightforward explanation to offer: our minds are not cognitively tuned to these problems. This is, as it were, just a piece of bad luck on our part, analogous to the lack of a language module in the brain of a dog. We make so little progress in philosophy for the same kind of reason we make so little progress in unassisted flying: we lack the requisite equipment. We have gaps in our cognitive skills as we have gaps in our motor skills – though in both cases we can see what we are missing and feel the resulting frustrations. That, for TN, is the kind of thing the hardness of philosophy consists in: not bewitchment by the surface forms of language, not deep implicitness in our conceptual scheme, not sheer meaninglessness, not objective complexity or intricacy or non-naturalness. None of these explanations would suit the case of the human inability to fly unaided, or to perceive ultraviolet light, or to hold ten thousand items in short-term memory; and TN holds that the kind of thing that explains these deficiencies is the kind of thing that makes us so poor at solving our philosophical problems.

Given this type of explanation, TN has a particular, and deflationary, account of our sense of philosophical depth. It is often supposed, if only tacitly, that the depth that philosophical questions appear to have is a reflection of some intrinsic feature of their subject-matter, difficult though it is to identify that feature in any illuminating way. TN opposes this tendency: it credits us with a propensity to commit a projective fallacy when we encounter a philosophical problem. We spread our own epistemic shortcomings onto the phenomena that perplex us, so raising the spectre of occult ontology. It then seems to us that the natural world contains metaphysical oddities, things whose very possibility comes into doubt. And hence philosophy takes on a semblance of special depth, as if it has to wrestle with facts of a peculiarly refractory nature, this impenetrability being grounded in objective reality. Philosophy is then apt to become a debate about whether there really are such facts after all. But TN counsels us to recognize this act of projection for what it is: we are mistaking a cognitive deficit on our part for an objective feature of what we are trying to understand. For a species gifted where we are deficient philosophical questions might have no more depth than we find in elementary geometry. In a sense, then, the depth is illusory, at least as a non-relative trait of the philosophical subject-matter. The predicate 'is philosophically deep', as applied to some worldly phenomenon, signifies a mind-dependent property, rather as the predicate 'is invisible at night' signifies a relation to some specific type of visual system. Indeed, the very concept of the philosophical, for TN, involves the idea of a problem that presents itself as a mystery, relative to some set of faculties of understanding. Creatures who understand our philosophical subject-matter with the ease we find in learning the simple properties of space and matter (say) would not reserve a special category of question labelled 'philosophy'. The word connotes a special kind of intellectual cramp or aura, and they are free of all that.

So far I have set out the TN view in an introductory way, trying to develop a feel for what it says; I have yet to offer any defence of it – a task to be undertaken in later chapters. But before I begin that task I need to introduce some further apparatus to be used in conjunction with TN. Again, we shall be proceeding abstractly, deferring applications till later.

III   Philosophical Geography

Philosophical debates tend to assume a characteristic pattern, with an array of options staked out and variously occupied. It will be useful for our purposes to identify this pattern, so that we can apply it in particular cases with TN in mind. The pattern may not always be clearly inscribed on the surface of debate, but I think it almost invariably lurks beneath. To this end, then, I shall introduce the DIME shape – the shape of the philosophical landscape as it is configured by the underlying how-possible questions. Consider a philosophically problematic concept C, with respect to which we wonder how it is possible that C should apply to the world; so we are going to need to do some philosophy on C if we are to understand what it is all about. Then the DIME shape displays four types of philosophical position that might be taken with respect to C, as follows.

D corresponds to the idea that C must be domesticated, demythologized, defanged, demoted, dessicated. Taken at face-value C presents large problems of understanding and integration, so in order to secure its objective possibility we need to redescribe it in some way. Simple reduction to a relatively unproblematic set of concepts is the standard manouevre here. The thought behind D is that C presents its referent in a misleading and inflated way, exaggerating its ontological uniqueness, so that we need to prune its pretensions somewhat. We must make C-facts humdrum and hence feasible. D may then incorporate an error thesis about C, either for an aspect of the concept itself or for the imaginative flights it provokes in us. However, the intentions of the D adherent are not to expel C-truths but to retain them, after some necessary wing-clipping. The position is that C-facts are really not so remarkable after all, upon a closer inspection of their content. Once unmasked, there is room for them at Nature's inn. They may seem set apart, but actually they are nothing but such-and-such innocent thing in disguise.

The I position is that C-facts are irreducible and indefinable and inexplicable, and we should cultivate an attitude of insouciance towards them. C-propositions state brute facts for which no explanation can be given and for which none should be sought; they are what they are and not another thing. D-style reductionism stems from misplaced monism, obsessive unification. We need to rid ourselves of the compulsion to oversimplify the world, to level it ontologically, and instead relax, indolently, into the *sui generis* variety of our given conceptual scheme. After all, it was functioning perfectly well before we started to fret over it. Apparent clashes between C and other beliefs we hold must result from mistaken philosophical theories or some slip in our thinking. Reality contains C-facts, and there's an end to it. Explanations must terminate at some point. C-facts are possible because they *are so*, and we can see that they are, irreducibly.

M stands for magical, miraculous, mystical . . . mad. The M believer accepts C-facts at face-value, unlike the D theorist, but he cannot simply take them as inexplicable, like the I adherent – he wants some account of their nature or basis. He seeks a larger picture of the world – a metaphysics – within which C-facts find an intelligible place. He is mightily impressed with C-facts, but he doubts they can be fitted into the natural order. His view is that the world is a stranger place than some people are prepared to admit. To make sense of it we need to invoke God or some equivalent supernatural entity of force. Reality thus includes more than the natural world; and it must, on pain of having no explanation of the facts. Only an M ontology can properly accommodate the data. C-facts are possible only because the world of science is not the only world there is. There are traces of the divine embedded in C. Indeed, the M believer is often to be found trying to establish the truth of a supernatural metaphysics on the basis of C-facts, by deduction or inference to the best explanation: for atoms in the void could never generate such remarkable facts. And even if the acceptance of an M position is less candid and enthusiastic than this, it can sometimes seem that nothing else will suffice: the philosopher may find himself driven in an M direction, perhaps concealing this move from himself, by the extreme difficulty of producing any coherent naturalistic account of the phenomenon in question. Indeed, we might say that the threat of M is partly definitive of a philosophical problem.

E is for elimination, ejection, extrusion. The E proponent despairs of domestication, balks at irreducibility, and scoffs at magic. His position is that C-facts look impossible because that is what they are: they are either prescientific remnants or logical absurdities of some sort. The entire C-ontology is an enormous illusion. C-talk should thus be banned, at least in serious contexts. The reason putative C-facts give us so much theoretical trouble is that we are trying to make sense of the non-existent. At best we might fashion a surrogate for them, to occupy their practical place, but in sober truth C-concepts have no application to the real world. Once we have eliminated them we can put all that distressing philosophical perplexity behind us. We can get on with more serious and workable pursuits, like natural science.

I assume this sketch of the philosophical lie of the land will not seem unfamiliar. Different philosophers at different times have found one or other position on the DIME shape attractive and settled on it. It is, I surmise, a common experience to find oneself moving from one location to another, as the demerits of that temporary resting-place make themselves felt. And there is a pattern to this dance – as D yields reluctantly to I, as I encourages a flirtation with M, as M propels one to E, as D seems like the place to try again. Plainly, too, E and D make natural partners, as do I and M. E is what opponents of D theorists accuse them of, and M is held to be the sub-text of the I adherent. It may not, in any particular case, be perfectly clear whether a given philosophical thesis is of the D or E variety, and similarly for its classification as I or M. E positions sometimes look like brazen versions of D positions, and M positions can seem like the logical conclusion of I positions. In any case, it should be clear enough for now how the philosophical choreography goes. It is a demanding piece, and it never seems to end.

We shall find this pattern repeatedly exemplified as we investigate the topics of the following chapters. And my thesis will be (a) that TN is a neglected alternative to any of the DIME positions and (b) that it is arguably preferable to those positions, especially for someone who already despairs (like me) of making good on a DIME-defined solution for philosophical problems. TN allows us to retain C-facts without underestimating or distorting them, without declaring them brutely inexplicable, and without courting ultimate mysteries in the world. We can thus escape E without being forced into any of the unsatisfactory positions to which E can seem the only way out. TN tells us how not to be eliminativists, while facing up to the deep and intractable problems C-facts pose to our modes of understanding. At the very least the TN option shows that it is a *non sequitur* to infer eliminativism from the failure of our epistemic faculties to comprehend what perplexes us. That would amount to the (idealist) fallacy of deriving an ontological conclusion from epistemological premisses. A better view, I shall suggest, is that the apparent

compulsoriness of the DIME dance results from systematically ig-
noring a TN position; so those who sense futility in that familiar
sequence of steps are released by TN from having to participate
therein.

IV   The CALM Conjecture

Ideally, TN needs to be accompanied by a worked-out theory of
human cognitive capacity, from which it would be demonstrable
that certain forms of understanding are not humanly accessible,
or run against the cognitive grain. This theory would be the
analogue for the faculty of reason (whatever precisely that means)
of a theory of the universal structure of human languages. That
latter theory, when taken as a description of the human language
faculty, contains principles that circumscribe the class of languages
accessible to the growing child, since the mind incorporates a
specialized language component that is selectively tuned to languages of the specified structure. Thus the grammar of human
languages determines the scope and limits of the human language
faculty, a particular organ of the mind.[11] What TN ideally requires, then, is something to play the role of grammar in delimiting
what is accessible to reason, where this something fixes boundaries
across which philosophical thought cannot travel. Needless to
say, I have nothing to offer that is even remotely comparable to
the present state of theorizing about the human language module;
but it is important that some stab should be made at saying what
at least such a theory would look like. So I shall now introduce
a framework for thought, to be deployed in the following chapters
and developed in chapter 8. The point now is just to get the basic
idea across, so that we shall have something with which to test
our intuitions in particular areas.

The CALM acronym stands for 'combinatorial atomism with
lawlike mappings'. This is intended to capture a certain mode of
thought, suited to certain subject-matters: that in which an array
of primitive elements is subject to specified principles of combination which generate determinate relations between complexes of
those elements. This combinatorial mode of thought, which yields
a certain kind of novelty in the domain at issue, and proceeds in

bottom-up style, may represent contemporaneous relations between the structures dealt with, as well as dynamic relations over time. The essence of it is to yield understanding of the domain, especially its generative aspects, by means of transparent relations of composition between elements: we can see, on the basis of a CALM theory, exactly how – by what principles – items in the domain of study are related to each other. Put differently, if we already know, pretheoretically, that there exist principled relations between these items, a CALM theory tells us what the nature of these relations is – it specifies the manner in which the domain is structured. To grasp the theory is thus to understand the domain.

Now I have stated the CALM idea in an intentionally abstract way, not mentioning any specific subject-matter which conforms to it. However, it is not difficult to cite areas of theory that pretty clearly exemplify the pattern: physics, linguistics and mathematics have a CALM character. I shall be brief about why this is so. In physics we deal with elements laid out in space and subject to aggregative operations; the resulting complexes (macroscopic material objects) are then governed by lawlike relations which map successive states of the physical world onto one another. Physical 'novelty' is a function of the aggregative rules and the laws of change over time.[12] In linguistics, too, we conceive our domain in terms of primitive elements (words, phonemes) that come together to form complex wholes, where the properties of the whole are projectible from properties of the elements and their principles of combination. Speech consists in the production of these complexes over time, with determinate linguistic relations between them. The aggregative rules here are formulated in a grammar – the rules of syntax and semantics. Linguistic novelty is then explained in terms of the combinatory rules and the primitives they operate on; on the basis of our grammatical theory, we can see how to generate novel linguistic structures. In mathematics geometry provides the most obvious illustration of the CALM format; indeed, one might well think of the CALM structure in general as the geometrical mode of thought transferred to other domains. In geometry, clearly, one works with geometrical primitives – lines, planes, volumes – and combines these into ever more complex structures, with precise rules laid out as to how geometrical objects are related. Theorems are proved on the basis of fundamental geometrical relations; the entire field has the kind of intelligible transparency we seek in understanding. But it is not just in the spatial (or quasi-spatial) parts of mathematics where CALM holds sway: number theory and set theory also fit the format. Elements and laws of combination prevail; mappings and functional relations abound; building up from the simple to the complex is ubiquitous. Spaces and structures and definable relations are what it is all about.

Of course, much more could be said in deepening and qualifying this abstract description of the fields mentioned, but I hope it is clear enough what the CALM idea is getting at. What will particularly concern me in what follows is a certain conjecture in which CALM features, namely that the philosophical problems we shall be dealing with resist resolution in CALM terms. We cannot dispel our perplexities by bringing to bear a CALM-style theory of the phenomena that puzzle us. The suggestion, then, tentatively made, will be that it is our conformity to CALM modes of thought that stands in the way of our achieving the kind of understanding we seek. That is the way our reason makes things intelligible to us, but in these cases the method breaks down, thus producing intractable puzzlement. In short, the CALM structure is to philosophical problems what human grammar is to nonhuman languages – an unavoidable but unsuitable mode of cognition. We apply the CALM mode willy-nilly to our problems, but instead of solving them it only steepens our sense of perplexity. That, at least, is to be the working conjecture.

V   Philosophy and Common Sense

Commonsense knowledge can be divided into two parts: knowledge of matter and knowledge of mind. We know the basic properties of things in space and how to negotiate these things practically, and we also know the basic properties of psychological beings and how to negotiate them practically. Both kinds of knowledge are exceedingly primitive, not in the sense that they are intrinsically simple, but in the sense that they condition our thought and action from an early age, and are acquired spontaneously. Higher animals share this kind of knowledge, suited to their given environment, and human children are in possession of it without benefit of explicit instruction. In many respects, the developmental characteristics of this knowledge mirror that of language: fragmentary data, rich system of knowledge, easy acquisition. It is thus highly plausible to suggest that commonsense knowledge has both an innate component and a modularized structure in the mind: the commonsense faculty has the kind of biological status attaching to the language faculty.[13] Nor is this surprising in view of what we know in general of the mind and given the evolutionary advantages of installing such knowledge in the organism's original endowment. Folk psychology, in particular, which will be our special concern, is plausibly viewed as a specialized subsystem of the mind, equipped with its own distinctive principles and programme of developmental expression, as well as a specific biological purpose. Let us, then, think of it as the mental equivalent of a physical organ of the body, with its own particular structure and function. Now we can ask how this cognitive organ might be related to the kind of reflective knowledge we seek in trying to do philosophy.

What is immediately striking, once one attends to it, is the enormous contrast that exists between the unreflective ease of acquisition of folk psychology, the ready manner in which we become adept in wielding it, and the extreme difficulty we experience in striving to make sense of, to explain, the basic ingredients of this knowledge-system. What came so easily to begin with cannot be made reflective sense of at maturity. It becomes as impenetrable as philosophy; in fact, it becomes philosophy. In the terms introduced earlier, we are programmed to employ concepts that are mysteries to us at a theoretical level. We can solve problems by *using* these concepts, but we cannot solve the problems they themselves raise – so says TN anyway. And this can seem surprising, for how can concepts that arose in us so smoothly be so resistant to reflective understanding?

The point I want to make is that this really should not seem so surprising once we have adopted the correct picture of the status of commonsense knowledge in the mind, and hence the truth of TN should not be seen as in any way paradoxical. Compare linguistic knowledge: would it be surprising if adult linguists proved unable to solve the theoretical problems posed by the output of the innate language faculty? No, because there is no a priori reason why the component of mind that yields ordinary linguistic knowledge should be penetrable by the components of mind that seek reflective theoretical knowledge: what one mental organ can do, and do readily, may not be capturable or replicable by means of other mental organs. Similarly, if folk-psychological knowledge arises in a specific component of the mind, possibly dissociable from other components, then it is entirely possible that the component we use when trying to do philosophy should be unable to get very far in developing theoretical knowledge of the output of the folk psychology faculty. Different components of mind enter into different cognitive tasks – language, common sense, science, mathematics, philosophy – and there is no general expectation that the concepts available to one component will be transferable to another. It may thus be that folk-psychological concepts are inherently resistant to the kind of theoretical understanding proper to the reflective faculties of mind. In trying to understand folk psychology we are bringing one mental organ to bear on another, but this may be as futile as trying to pump the blood with the kidneys. Less colourfully put, on a modular view of human cognitive capacity, TN is by no means surprising, since it says merely that what comes easily to one faculty, for its limited purposes, may altogether defy the efforts of another faculty with *its* limited purposes. There is thus nothing very remarkable in the idea that we may not be able to understand the presuppositions of our own concepts. These presuppositions may simply not be the business of the common sense faculty, and they may not be accessible to the reflective faculties. It is not that somehow we *ought* to be able to answer the questions our commonsense concepts raise, if only we put in more effort.[14]

Still, if this is right, it does provide some account of the teasing, and even shaming, quality that philosophical puzzlement is sometimes felt to have. The problematic concepts enter our thought processes with great ease, but when we reflect on them we encounter deep difficulties. This can be felt as mildly embarrassing: we must be pretty dense to have so much trouble making articulate sense of what children pick up without a second thought. But actually, if the present picture is right, there is no reason for self-castigation: it is just that the contents of one module are not explicable in the terms proper to another. It is not so very different from being unable to explain the physical workings of one's own body. So there is no real paradox in the idea that folk psychology is both remarkably easy and impossibly hard. Nor should it be simply assumed that philosophy can supply a theoretical vindication of common sense, if this means give an intelligible account of the place of commonsense facts in the world. Philosophy and common sense belong to different regions of the human mind, which may be related only tenuously.[15]

Let me make clear the scope of my aims in this book. I am not intending to discuss every question we dub 'philosophical'; I shall be dealing with a certain set of central questions, mainly relating to the mind. Whether the approach can be extended beyond this (already ambitious) set I shall not enquire. There is, of course, no necessity that every question discussed in departments of philosophy should be of the same underlying kind: intellectual natural kinds are not fixed by institutional demarcations. I do think, however, that the questions to be discussed in what follows do naturally belong together, so that a unified approach, metaphilosophically, is a sensible project. When I speak of 'philosophy', then, I should be understood as referring to this batch of questions, and possibly any others of the same type; it is of no concern to me that philosophers may in fact discuss questions for which TN is clearly inappropriate, or that nonphilosophers might discuss questions for which it is (say, physicists).

The topics that will occupy us in the ensuing chapters include consciousness, personhood, freedom, intentionality, knowledge. These notions are all embedded deep in folk psychology, so our general question is whether TN is the right perspective to take on such folk-psychological notions. Are the ultimate natures of the phenomena so signified open to our theoretical understanding? Are our own minds in principle intelligible to us?

NOTES

1   I am here following Noam Chomsky: see *Reflections on Language*, chapter 4, and *Language and Problems of Knowledge*, chapter 5.

2 This remains the case even if *any* mind (in some sufficiently well-defined sense) is incapable of answering the question at issue, since no ontological consequences follow from universal incapacity of this kind. It is still a point about *minds* – not the objective world – that they cannot, and cannot essentially, answer a certain type of question.

3 On mental organs and cognitive structure see Chomsky, *Rules and Representations*, chapter 1.

4 'Non-natural' is a catch-all term, encompassing a variety of philosophical trends, ranging from the explicitly God-invoking, to the 'queer processes' Wittgenstein speaks of, to certain kinds of ethical and mathematical realism. Not much weight should be placed on the intended general notion. TN is profoundly suspicious of the whole natural/non-natural contrast – except insofar as it characterizes the phenomenology of philosophical thought. What exists does so without impediment or metaphysical inharmony: it simply is.

5 For a defence of this kind of realism see Thomas Nagel, *The View From Nowhere*, chapter 6.

6 Again, this is a Chomskian thesis: see *Rules and Representations*, chapters 2 and 3. To be biased in favour of the universal grammar specific to human languages is, *eo ipso*, to be biased against grammars that diverge from this – richness in one direction going along with poverty in another (and contrariwise).

7 Of course, so-called *tabula rasa* conceptions of mind ultimately differ from structured conceptions only in degree, since no sense can be made of the idea of a wholly structureless cognitive system – any more than that of a formless physical object. Still, even if all minds were to share the same intrinsic nature, some problems might exceed the capacities of every such mind, thus generating cognitive closure without cognitive differentiation.

8 Remember, however, that such cognitive deficits are apt to be the inevitable outcome of cognitive strengths along other dimensions: we are bad at philosophy *because* we are good at something else – rather as we are bad at breathing under water because we are good at breathing in the open air.

9 Analytic philosophy, as a metaphilosophical position, is thus premissed on the assumption that the nature of certain objective facts is coded into the concepts we bring to those facts, so that philosophical truth is to be ascertained quite differently from other kinds of truth – as it were, by gazing into the conceptual mirror in which reality is reflected. This is actually, when you think about it, a very surprising and radical idea – by no means the platitude

its familiarity suggests. For why *should* certain parts of reality, and not others, be thus coded? Certainly this does not follow from the admission that *some* conceptual clarification is always part of philosophical enquiry. What is rather needed is the startling idea that some objective phenomena have already yielded up their inner nature to the human conceptual scheme – an idea that can hardly be regarded as axiomatic.

10 The distinction between science and philosophy, which is relatively recent in intellectual history, is, for TN, largely an artifact of the epistemic capacities we bring to bear on our problems: 'science' is simply the name we apply to questions that fit our theoretical faculties, while 'philosophy' denotes questions that do not. Strictly speaking, then, science never slices off what is properly called philosophy, i.e. that which has the kind of special hardness of which TN has an account. What happened historically was, in effect, that certain questions traditionally labelled 'philosophy' were seen to differ from others in point of their intellectual accessibility. So the history of thought can be seen as a kind of map of the human cognitive system, depicting its powers and limitations.

11 See Chomsky, *Rules and Representations*, chapter 6.

12 Of course, I am oversimplifying the content of extant physical theories, in all their exotic glory. My point is not that everything in physics is unmysterious because physics is comprehensively CALM; it is, rather, that physical concepts and theories are unmysterious *in proportion* as they have a CALM interpretation – and they fundamentally do. Quantum physics is theoretically problematic, at least in certain respects, just because it fails of CALM interpretation. Newton's original sense of the unacceptably occult character of the gravitational force, in contrast to other aspects of his theory, might be thought to have a similar source, since that force cannot be construed in terms of the rearrangement of constituent elements in a suitable medium. It is no part of TN, as I intend it, to assert that nothing outside what is commonly designated 'philosophy' presents problems of understanding comparable to those that typify philosophical questions of the kind I shall be discussing. So-called foundational issues in the sciences might well tap into the same biases and deficits that generate what we think of as philosophical perplexity. In general, the interesting distinctions here do not necessarily coincide with the usual institutional demarcations.

13 For a discussion see Jerry Fodor, *Psychosemantics*, epilogue.

14 Note that chimps possess commonsense psychological knowledge, useful in organizing their social relations, but lack the reflective

capacities we enjoy; so they cannot appreciate the problems raised by their own scheme of psychological concepts. They share one of our modules but not the other. Perhaps in the fullness of time they will evolve a reflective capacity, less developed than ours, and then become puzzled about their concepts; but we will not expect them to be able to lay their puzzlement to rest just because they are now equipped to feel it.

15 It is important here to distinguish between two vindicating projects: on the one hand, to protect common sense from philosophical perplexity; on the other, to answer such perplexity by producing a *theory* of common sense notions. TN says that the second project is impossible, but it refuses to infer that common sense should be abandoned, since it interprets the impossibility purely epistemically – so it serves in the less ambitious vindicating project. TN offers what I have elsewhere called a 'nonconstructive' vindication of common sense: see *The Problem of Consciousness*.

2

Consciousness

I The Problem: Consciousness and the Brain

Consciousness undoubtedly exists: it has the status of a datum, not a dispensable theoretical construct. But it ought not to be possible at all, given what we know of human and animal bodies, for there seems nothing about physical organisms from which it could conceivably arise. Physical states of the organism are, to all appearances, *de facto* necessary and sufficient conditions for conscious states, and the brain is surely centrally implicated, but electrochemical impulses travelling along nerve strands seem far removed from what they somehow secure. The operations of matter look like a singularly inadequate foundation for a mental life – a plan for making conscious states that stands no chance of success. It is thus numbingly difficult to make sense of the fact of material emergence, since nothing plausible suggests itself as an adequate basis for getting consciousness off the ground. Intelligibility expires in the explanatory vacuum that confronts us. We have something like physical supervenience, but this only accentuates the explanatory problem rather than solving it, since the supervenience appears brute and unmediated. We have no conception of what a unifying theory of consciousness and matter would look like. The resulting logical gulf presents us with a deep mystery: how does the world contrive to do what we cannot conceive of it as doing? That is the mind–body problem – finding an explanatory theory of the psychophysical link that will enable us to resolve the mysteries the data present.

This is a simple and pure form of the kind of problem characteristic of philosophical perplexity. Common sense (perhaps
augmented with a bit of science) tells us that something is the
case, but we have the greatest difficulty in developing a conception of the world that will allow us to accept what common sense
tells us. It can then appear that we shall be compelled to revise
common sense, on pain of absurdity in our conceptual system, or
metaphysical conjuring tricks in objective reality. Consciousness
puzzles us in a special way – the way we label 'philosophical': it
is quite unlike our puzzlement over (say) how salt dissolves in
water or plants grow.[1] The head spins in theoretical disarray; no
explanatory model suggests itself; bizarre ontologies loom. There
is a feeling of intense confusion, but no clear idea about where
the confusion lies. It is also a puzzlement that is easier to experience
than to formulate, since it is exceedingly difficult to say precisely
what it is about consciousness that makes it so uncongenial to physical explanation. Our intuitions outrun our diagnostic powers –
in a way that is also characteristic of philosophical bewilderment.
Something is wrong somewhere, deeply so, but even putting one's
finger on it can prove testing. Hence there exist philosophers who
deny (with eyes studiously averted) that there is any real problem
about consciousness.

In this chapter I shall apply the apparatus introduced in the
previous chapter to the problem of consciousness. This should
serve to make that apparatus more concrete, as well as to shed
light on the particular problem at hand. My further aim is to
treat that problem as a philosophical paradigm, approaching the
later problems with this as a model and guide. First we shall see
how TN applies to the mind–body problem; then we shall extend
it into neighbouring areas of philosophical aporia.

Let me begin, though, with matters of formulation, so that we
are as clear as we can be about what we are asking; a little
preliminary pedantry may ease some of the murkiness of the
topic. What, then, is the mark of a conscious state? Where precisely is the problem located? A celebrated stab at encapsulating
the property of consciousness that eludes physical explanation
introduces the phrase, 'what it is like to be a K'.[2] This is intended
to capture the intrinsic non-relational essence of the conscious
state, the aspect that distinguishes it from states that may share

a similar set of extrinsic relational properties. To satisfy such a description is to enjoy subjective states, states which exist *for* a subject. Now this is certainly an apt locution, but it can mislead, so let me warn against some possible misconstruals of it.

First, let us attend to questions of logical scope. Consider the sentence, 'there is something it is like to be a bat': this contains two quantifier expressions, at the beginning and end. The first, 'there is something', is best taken as second-order, ranging over properties that bats may instantiate, so that the entire sentence can be cumbrously parsed as 'there is some property P such that bats have P and P confers "likeness" on bats'. P is a subjective property of bats, in contrast to bat properties that confer no 'likeness' on them. In any case, we are quantifying over a type not a token, a universal not a particular: no conscious token confers any 'likeness' beyond that conferred by its conscious type. The second quantifier phrase, 'a bat', is plainly first-order and ranges, universally, over individual bats. We have to be careful about the relative scopes of the two quantifiers if we are to read the vernacular phrase in the intended way. The claim is not that, concerning any individual bat x, there is something it is like to be x; the claim is rather that there is something it is like to be any bat at all. The subjective property is not tied to the particular bat we happen to be considering but encompasses all (normal) bats. It is not that being a *particular* conscious subject has its own unique subjective type, so that mine might be different from yours simply in virtue of our numerical distinctness; rather, my subjectivity is shared by any being relevantly similar to me. Phenomenologies are not individuated by numerical identity; they concern qualitative identity. So there is no suggestion here that the problem of subjectivity has to do with distinguishing one individual subject from another (though this latter is a real problem in its own right, of course). It is about the experience-type common to the generality of bats (say).[3]

That was a fairly straightforward point; the next one cannot be sorted out quite so crisply. It concerns the notion of what a certain experience-type is like *for* its subject. It is tempting to read the phrase as suggesting that there is a way that *being* a bat is for a bat – a way bat experience strikes bats. On this understanding, we are saying that the experiences are presented to the bats in a certain way, that bats take their experiences as objects of apprehension; and thus the subjective character of experience is held to consist in how experiences appear to something like introspection. And if that is so, then the bats must somehow represent their own experiences to themselves, bringing them under higher-order intentional states. They must possess states whose content refers to the experiences delivered by their sonar sense; and it is the possession of these states that constitutes subjectivity.

Clearly, something is going wrong here. We don't want to credit bats with higher-order representational states, i.e. self-reflection; or if we do, it is not merely because we think their sensations have subjective character. For surely sensations have a subjective aspect whether or not their subjects can reflect on them and acknowledge this fact. What is presented to the bat in a specific subjective way, when its sonar sense operates, are things in the external world, the environmental objects it perceives by means of that sense. What it is like to *be* a bat is identical with what the *world* is like for a bat. The bat's subjectivity consists in the particular way in which the perceived environment appears to the bat, not in how those perceptions themselves appear to it. The only intentional contents here represent external objects, but the manner of this representation confers a subjective character on the perceptual experiences that bear this outer-directed content. Thus in the specification of the bat's subjectivity the only intentional relation involved holds between the bat and the world, not between the bat and its own experience *of* the world. It is a matter of how those rebounding high-pitched sounds appear to the bat. In other terms, it is a matter of the secondary qualities associated with the bat's sonar sense.[4]

Then we can formulate our perplexity about consciousness as follows: how is it possible for states which there is something it is like to have to arise out of states of a kind which there is nothing it is like to have? The physical states that correlate with conscious states – neural firings of certain frequencies – look, on their surface, to be states of a kind that can occur in the total absence of consciousness; indeed, there seems nothing about them that could explain why *those* states, rather than (say) states of the kidneys, are the basis of consciousness. One could never tell, just by inspecting brain states, that they are uniquely the source of consciousness; this is something we know only by independently established correlations. It is as if *any* kind of physical state could have turned out to be the basis of consciousness; it just happens that it is neurons and their peculiar activities. Thus there is an irreducible bruteness to the correlation, as if consciousness has just been *pasted on* to the cerebral material. By some unknown process, electrochemical events give rise to states which there is something it is like to have: a subject of awareness is bodied forth from raw materials that look remarkably unsuitable for the job (not that we have any idea what other sorts of materials would be cut out for the job). The problem is essentially architectural: how would you set about constructing subjective states from the cellular structures that compose the brain? Until we have some idea how to answer that, and in particular some grasp of the architectural principles involved, as we do for other biological traits and organs, we are faced with a gaping explanatory hole in our theory of how the world works. That hole is called 'the mind–body problem'.[5]

II DIME and Consciousness

My programme, I said, is to illustrate the DIME alternatives using consciousness as a philosophical paradigm, and then proceed on this basis to other topics. I shall not be attempting to show, in this chapter or later ones, that the range of DIME positions philosophers have entertained is inadequate to the problems; this is indeed my opinion, but I do not expect to establish it here. Brief surveys must suffice, accompanied by tendentious indications of where the weaknesses lie. Adherents of these positions cannot expect to be persuaded out of their convictions. I speak, rather, to those who are similarly dissatisfied with the usual sorts of positions and would like to see a way out. There is, I believe, a systematic pattern to philosophical disputation, in which the same kinds of unsatisfying alternatives recur; the point of TN is to break the hold of this pattern, by supplying a better alternative and by making metaphilosophical sense of the usual dialectic. The tone, then, will be diagnostic rather than refutative. So: into what kinds of (contorted!) posture has consciousness driven philosophers, past and present?

Domesticating programmes are familiar enough – attempts to convince us that consciousness is really nothing more than such-and-such. When you analyse conscious states sufficiently the specialness dissolves. Consciousness can be reduced to facts of a metaphysically unproblematic kind. Materialism and functionalism are the most obvious D positions today: to be in a conscious state is just to be in a certain sort of physical state – a neural state or a state defined by causal role.[6] The spookiness is an illusion, to be dispelled by acquiring more physical knowledge of the kind we already possess. Our conceptual scheme already contains the essential resources for a comprehensive theory of consciousness. Also to be included under this heading are such ideas as that consciousness is just a kind of self-monitoring or higher-order belief state or criterionless self-ascription;[7] or again, that it is simply one kind of emergent biological property among others, raising no deeper question than that raised by the nature of digestion or the like.[8] D positions thus take something relatively common-place and well-understood, something less mysterious-seeming, and assert that consciousness can be explained in those terms. The solution to the mind–body problem is then consequent on this assimilation.

The standard and oft-repeated objection to such positions is simply that they fail to do justice to the facts: it is just not plausible that consciousness is nothing more than the things that are thus held to constitute it. The reductions miss something out, the essence indeed. This general intuition is then often backed up with specific objections, which typically have less power than the general sense of inadequacy: that the psychophysical link is more contingent than these theories allow;[9] that specific aspects of phenomenology elude explanations of these kinds;[10] that we can imagine creatures who satisfy the reductive conditions yet lack any consciousness at all.[11] In short, domestication is tantamount to denial, to defying the data.

Irreducibility theses suggest themselves when once the prospects for domestication dim. If consciousness cannot be reduced to something familiar, that must be because it is intrinsically irreducible – ontologically basic, an explanatory terminus. Accordingly, we must accept that psychophysical correlations, biological emergence and physical supervenience are all simply brute facts, admitting of no explanation. The nature of consciousness is already fully represented in our ordinary concepts, and it is only an exaggerated explanatory urge that makes us think our theories of the world have any essential incompleteness. It is simply an inexplicable fact that irreducible conscious states have the kinds of relations to the physical world that they have. There is nowhere deeper to dig; the world has no ontological complexity beyond that recorded in our ordinary descriptions of things. Mental properties have no internal intelligible relation to physical properties, despite their dependence on such properties. We must accept the duality without perplexing ourselves about its possibility.[12]

Here the objection is apt to be that brute irreducibility, while paying ample respect to the *sui generis* character of conscious states, does so only at the cost of rendering their place in the world unacceptably mysterious; it thus abnegates our explanatory responsibilities. What is it about neural tissue in particular that makes *it* capable of subserving conscious states? Would we be content with the claim that consciousness emerges from sawdust quite inexplicably? Are we not mistaking human ignorance for ontological basicness? The leap from matter to mind is surely too great to be totally unmediated; it must be backed by natural principles of some kind. And if, as seems plausible, there are objective necessities at work in tying consciousness to the physical world, there must be some account of these necessities; it isn't merely accidental or adventitious that the brain is the organ of consciousness. Coincidences may not need explanation, but it is surely no coincidence that brain tissue and conscious processes go systematically together. Irreducibility theses are culpably silent on such questions. They leave consciousness hanging.[13]

Miracle theses have tended to lapse in these secular times, at least in scientific circles, but they were more or less orthodox until relatively recently. They may be divided into theses in which a divine being is brought in to underwrite the miracle and theses in which the miracle is taken as ultimate. Of course, it is quite unclear that this notion of objective miracle is even coherent, but that is not sufficient to deter people from subscribing to ideas framed in these terms. The thought (or attempted thought) is that the world is not fully intelligible in terms of causes, laws, mechanisms, natural forces; there are ultimate anomalies out there, contraventions of the naturalistic viewpoint. God plays tricks with nature, or nature plays tricks with itself. Thus we have the traditional idea of the soul, an immaterial particle (sic) floating somewhere above the flux of physical events. It owes its being to nothing (except perhaps God), it is immortal, and it can recur in subsequent lives. Its interaction with the body is miraculous, quite possibly requiring God's continual intervention. It belongs to that order of reality in which angels and ghosts and miraculous healings occur. It is not of this world. You get goosepimples just thinking about it! It is futile to try to explain it in sublunary terms; its nature is to flout nature. It is, precisely, *super*natural. Consciousness is the divine spark in each of us.

I take M positions seriously, not as genuine candidates for truth, but as expressive of the philosophical hysteria that so readily envelops us. What is interesting is that we can find ourselves uttering these words, or falling inchoately into these thoughts. For it is doubtful that any of this really means anything. It is mere poetry, rhetoric, word-spinning. Falsity is not the main problem, though doubtless there is some of that; the problem rather is that of coherence, of staking out a genuine position in logical space. What could it *mean* to say that consciousness is supernatural? What content does the notion of the supernatural really have? Still, radically defective as M positions no doubt are, they exercise a powerful hold on speculative reason, so we must include them among the responses that philosophical problems provoke. They play their part in defining the options to which thinkers resort in contemplating the mind–body problem (among other things). And showing how to avoid adopting an incoherent position is often a substantive philosophical task. Indeed, one of the chief merits of TN is that it allows us to dismiss all such intimations as by-products of our principled ignorance on the matter, faltering steps into the epistemic abyss.[14]

Eliminative theses may be regarded as positions of last resort. When D ambitions have been abandoned, and I declarations have come to sound hollow, and M creeds have been forsworn, *then* it starts to seem compulsory to reject the thing that generates the problem. Boldy one asserts: there is *no such thing* as consciousness. One undertakes to eliminate it from one's ontology; one encases talk of it in inverted commas. By so denying its very existence one sidesteps the mind–body problem altogether: that problem is the pseudo-problem of trying to link a mythical realm to sober reality. If there were such a thing as consciousness, it would have to be magical; but there is no magic in the world, so neither is there consciousnes. Less extremely put, there is no room for consciousness in our emerging scientific view of the world; and what resists scientific integration had better be eliminated altogether.[15]

The usual response to eliminative theses is plain incredulity: to deny that one is concious requires one to deny what is self-evident. It is not like denying the existence of vital spirits or the devil, since conscious states are *data* – part of what the world presents to us as simply so. Moreover, to cease to talk in terms of consciousness would be to cripple our entire conception of ourselves and one another. E theses are in the position of rejecting the obvious because no good theory of it can be found.

Thus it is that the DIME shape stamps itself onto the topic of consciousness. Now we shall ask how TN responds to the problem.

III TN and Consciousness

TN with respect to consciousness is this claim: the natural principles which mediate between brain processes and conscious states are inaccessible to human reason. We would need a conceptual revolution in order to solve the mind–body problem, but it is not a revolution our intellects can effect. It is a general trait of organisms to have areas of cognitive strength and weakness, and the human cognitive system is weak precisely where the problem of consciousness arises. The requisite theory does not come within the scope of our mental modules.

According to TN, the DIME shape characterizes philosophical debate about the mind–body problem precisely because of the truth of TN. D projects tempt us, and predictably fail, because we try to force conscious phenomena into a conceptual mould that ill suits them, striving to bring them under a set of theoretical notions that is available to us – but actually doesn't fit the facts. The correct theory lies to the side of what we can generate, so we make do with theories that at best approximate to the truth. I positions attract us because no accessible theory offers any explanatory hope, so we rush to deny that any such theory exists – thus fallaciously deducing an ontological conclusion from premisses about human epistemology. M doctrines are hyperbolic responses to the (epistemically) mysterious character of consciousness: they are reifications of our own cognitive limitations. And E conclusions are panicky attempts to remedy what is ultimately an epistemological problem: if we cannot understand it, even in principle, then we are prone to deny that it exists. In that way we can protect ourselves from the unflattering truth that parts of nature will not yield their secrets to the human cognitive apparatus.[16] The organ sitting in our heads has not the size and power to comprehend everything that exists.

Thus TN predicts that the DIME shape will imprint itself on the mind–body problem, but it denies that DIME exhausts our options. And in so far as those options are admitted to be unsatisfactory, TN offers itself as a preferable alternative. It is, at the very least, a hypothesis worth taking seriously; a factual hypothesis, indeed, about the structure and scope of human understanding, to be evaluated as empirical hypotheses generally are. What, we should ask, is its antecedent likelihood, given the general nature of evolved cognitive systems; and what evidence from the field of human enquiry might speak in its favour?

Now I have defended TN about the mind-brain link at some length in *The Problem of Consciousness*,[17] and I do not propose to repeat here everything I said there. My aims now are more illustrative: I want to use the mind–body problem to exemplify the general metaphilosophical position I am exploring, and to provide a paradigm for other philosophical problems. Let me then quote a remarkable passage from the nineteenth-century scientist John Tyndall, which succinctly expresses the spirit of the TN position: 'The passage from the physics of the brain to the corresponding facts of consciousness is unthinkable. Granted that a definite thought and a definite molecular action in the brain occur simultaneously, we do not possess the intellectual organ, nor apparently any rudiment of the organ, which would enable us to pass, by a process of reasoning, from one to the other'.[18] This gets it exactly right by my lights, even down to the suggestion of an explanation of the unthinkability in terms of mental modularity. My general thesis, in these terms, is that philosophical bafflement results from the lack of an 'intellectual organ' suitable to the subject. I would only add, what Tyndall leaves implicit, that the unthinkability is no reason to suppose that anything supernatural or intrinsically brute is going on: this is strictly a point about how our intellects are constituted, not a comment on the miraculous doings of the real world. That *we* cannot make the explanatory passage from brain to mind does not entail that the *brain* exercises any magical function in so doing. Epistemic limits never entail ontological fissures or fishiness.

Can we give more colour to this idea of organ lack? What is it about our modes of thought and our access to the phenomena that generates the closure TN detects? Here we can do little more than point to clues, speculatively interpreting what we find. I shall mention two points, both suggestive rather than apodictic; this should at least tell us the *kind* of thing we should be seeking in diagnosing the truth of TN. The first point concerns CALM, the second a particular property of introspection.

It is a familiar thought that conscious states resist emergent explanation in terms of mereological notions: that is, we cannot think of pains (say) as aggregates of the neural units that underlie them, either cells or the firings thereof. By contrast, higher-level properties of liquids (say) can be construed in terms of lower-level constituents and their combinatorial possibilities: so we understand the relation (supervenience, in effect) between the higher-level properties and the underlying matrix of combining molecules. This is, in my terms, a pure case of CALM understanding: atomic elements combining according to certain laws and mapping intelligibly onto the facts to be explained – parts and wholes, basically. But this is just what we are prevented from doing in the case of consciousness and the brain: conscious states are not CALM-construable products of brain components. Here the mappings, which must exist in some form, are inscrutable in CALM terms. We can readily conceive of higher-level brain functions in terms of simpler composing constituents; but once we think in terms of consciousness this mode of explanation lapses. Thus we have no model of what the emergence relation might consist in; here the supervenience is opaque and puzzling, not transparent and intelligible. Similarly, it seems quite unpromising to adopt a more syntactic CALM explanation: even if there are symbols in the brain, conscious states are not explicable as mere syntactic strings of such symbols. If conscious states have something like constituent structure, that lies at the conscious level itself; it is not a way of levering consciousness out of brain properties. Given that the CALM format governs our conception of natural emergence, it is no surprise that consciousness should be so baffling to us. We have a CALM bias, but we cannot implement this in explaining the mind–brain link. TN takes this to be symptomatic of the closure it alleges.

The second point concerns what I have elsewhere called the hidden structure of consciousness.[19] The basic idea is that conscious states conceal a hidden nature that enables them to hook onto brain states. Now this notion of the hidden is to be interpreted purely epistemically, as a point about the faculties we bring to bear in apprehending conscious states; it is not meant to be some kind of objective occlusion, as with tree roots buried under ground. So we can ask what properties of our consciousness-apprehending faculties might generate this kind of partial access. And there is a feature that is at least suggestive, which I shall call the 'single-channel' property of introspection. Let us agree that the scope of a cognitive faculty is constrained by its pattern of causal sensitivities: what it can represent is a function of the properties it can causally resonate to. This implies that the more fixed and invariant the causal dependence between states of the faculty and states of its (intentional) objects the less the faculty will tell us about those objects, other things being equal. If a faculty is operationally tied to a single perspective on an object, then it is unlikely to yield the whole nature of that on which it has this fixed perspective. My hypothesis, then, is that introspection is a highly restricted and rigid epistemic resonator; it is a single-channel faculty, confined to a mere subset of the properties of its objects. We do not enjoy a rich variety of modes of apprehension of conscious states, analogous to the five senses we bring to the external world, and the single mode we do have is notably inflexible in its operation. Compare vision or touch, which provide multiple causal channels onto their objects, corresponding to shifts of position and focus and so on. If we want to know about the properties of a chair, say, we can explore it from many points of view, using sight and touch, revealing new aspects as we proceed. Thus we develop a rich conception of its nature, and science becomes possible. But introspection does not similarly provide for a rich conception of its objects. If we want to know about a pain, there is little we can do but detect its presence by simple introspection. We cannot shift viewpoint or bring to bear another sense. We quickly run out of things to say about our conscious states because introspection tells us so few things about them. It is a bit like trying to discover the full nature of a chair with only vision and one's eyes permanently fixed two inches away from the surface of one of the arms! At any rate, that is the hypothesis we are entertaining. The thought then is that we should not be surprised that consciousness has a hidden nature, postulated for theoretical reasons, once we notice that our faculties of self-knowledge are trained upon it in such a restricted and uniform way. Introspection is remarkably effective in employing its single mode of access to detect *some* properties of conscious states, but this very fact makes it inept at developing a rounded picture of the objects on which it reports. Its operational principles do not suit it for revealing all the interesting properties of conscious states. Again, TN sees in this a (partial) rationale for the deep ignorance that afflicts our understanding of the phenomena. We can begin to see why the closure conjectured by TN should not be exclaimed over – it is a natural upshot of constitutive facts about the faculties that are relevant to the problem. Closure is not, of course, *proven* by these facts, but they do serve to make sense out of an acknowledged futility.

There is, after all, no a priori reason to suppose that the nature of consciousness is fully revealed to conscious beings themselves. On the contrary, consciousness was presumably designed chiefly as a vehicle of mental representation, not as an object of it: its job is primarily to act as a medium of thought and perception, specifically in respect of the external world. But when we try to form representations *of* consciousness, making the vehicle into its own object, we encounter a notable paucity: our concepts of consciousness do not lead the way into a developed science of consciousness. It is, as it were, a good object-language but an indifferent meta-language, lacking the resources to describe itself with any degree of depth. Just as a natural language could express extensive knowledge of the world without having much to say about itself, so consciousness, as a medium of intentionality, seems pretty powerful about what lies outside it but provides little or nothing in the way of real theory about its own nature. This is obvious enough for the simpler conscious organisms, whose reflexive representations are minimal indeed, and there is no reason to suppose that human beings are in a qualitatively different case. As ordinary speakers lack rational mastery of linguistic theory, so conscious subjects lack a theory of consciousness; and we should not be terribly surprised if the lack is permanent, in view of the structure and function of the system.

IV   Sense, Reference and the Mind–Body Problem

Using the sense/reference distinction, TN about the mind–body problem can be stated thus: brain states and conscious states fall under senses such that (i) under those senses the link between them is intelligible and (ii) those senses are not potential constituents of human thoughts. That is, the references of mental and cerebral terms have aspects, corresponding to (ideal) senses, which provide the kind of natural nexus we cannot, under our present concepts, envisage. We might say that these senses are the mystery-resolving senses for the philosophical mind–body problem; they correspond to the kind of conceptual shift that would render the psychophysical relation transparent, *if* it could be achieved. They occur in the propositions that constitute the (ideal) scientific theory of mind and body. And they are not identical with the senses we now associate with our terms; indeed, they must be far removed from these senses – though presumably some explanatory link has to hold between the two. If we imagine creatures whose cognitive structure allows them to incorporate the mystery-resolving senses into their thoughts, then we can say that for these creatures there is no aura of impenetrable mystery surrounding the psychophysical link. For them, the connexion is as unmysterious as any other natural nexus, a matter of plain science. TN thus diagnoses the character of the philosophical problem for us as consisting in the cognitive inaccessibility of the right senses, the ones that convert the problem into regular science.

On this conception, then, no *reference* ever in itself poses a philosophical problem: the objective world is philosophically unproblematic. Philosophical problems arise from the senses under which we conceive the world; they are, in one good sense, purely conceptual problems. By varying the senses we can transform a question from philosophy to non-philosophy, as when we imagine creatures whose modes of conception present them with no philosophical mystery; and we can do the converse too. Whether a question counts as philosophical depends upon who is doing the philosophizing, i.e. what conceptual and theoretical resources they possess: that is the point of TN. In the case of the mind–body problem, the mystery exists only for creatures whose cognitive slant biases them away from the concepts that are needed to make the question into a mere scientific problem. The mystery does not attach to the reference of mental terms *no matter* how this reference might be presented to a creature.

The point of my restating the TN position in these terms is to raise the following issue: is there such a thing as a *philosophical* answer to a philosophical question? And, given what has just been said, the reply would seem to be in the negative. For an answer to a philosophical question is a proposition, referring to the entities originally puzzled over, which contains senses that generate no peculiarly philosophical perplexity. Let us call this a 'scientific' proposition: then we can say that the answer to the mind–body problem consists in a set of scientific propositions, not humanly accessible according to TN, that are such that *were* they to be grasped by some being they would produce no sense of philosophical mystery in that being. They would have the same kind of epistemic status that the propositions of human science have. So the philosophical mind–body problem does not have a peculiarly *philosophical* answer; the theory that resolves the problem is not a distinctively philosophical theory. And in so far as this problem is a paradigm for other problems, they too lack distinctively philosophical solutions. If a class of creatures found digestion philosophically problematic, by dint of a conceptual lack that we simply take for granted, then the answer to their puzzlement would be a straight scientific theory of digestion, not some peculiarly philosophical theory of the nature of digestion. That is how TN views the human epistemic predicament with respect to our (so-called) philosophical problems. We have philosophical questions, individuated by the senses we bring to our terms, but these questions do not have philosophical answers – except in so far as they answer philosophical questions. Knowledge of the world, including the parts of it that produce philosophical puzzlement in human beings, is all of a piece; where obtainable it all forms a continuous fabric of understanding. There is not philosophical knowledge on the one hand and scientific knowledge on the other. It only seems that this is so because of the deep partition among questions that results from our cognitive biases. In a sense, then, TN does not believe in philosophy as a separate discipline. There is, to be sure, such a thing as philosophical ignorance, but there is no such thing as philosophical knowledge – not as traditionally conceived. Put less grandly, the mind–body problem (for example) has a merely scientific solution, but it seems to us like a peculiarly philosophical problem because the requisite theory lies outside of our cognitive bounds. Thinking of the matter in terms of sense and reference can help to clarify what is going on here. In a slogan: philosophical problems attach to the level of sense not to the level of reference.

I doubt that many readers will feel persuaded of this claim at the present stage of the discussion, either generally or for the specific case of consciousness; but it should at least be coming clear what the claim is and what motivates it. My persuasive intentions are cumulative: assent at any one point will depend upon the appeal of the larger picture, upon the overall pattern that emerges from a number of areas. Does the TN hypothesis make things fall generally into place? For we are dealing here with a family of problems, interlinked in various ways, and what we say about any one of them will have a bearing on the right view of the others. We need a global perspective if TN is to be properly evaluated in more local contexts.

Two big links should be borne in mind from now on. First, TN with respect to the mind–body problem may be bolstered by considering connected areas in which a similar view appears plausible. I suspect that many people believe that the mind–body problem is in principle soluble in terms of future human science, and that I exaggerate our cognitive blankness on the question. Such people may, however, be less inclined to this kind of optimism (or lack of pessimism) with respect to certain other philosophical problems I shall discuss, say the self or free will or meaning; so considering consciousness in conjunction with these may instill some doubts about its accessibility to future scientific understanding. For the question will need to be addressed as to why the consciousness problem is more tractable than those others, especially in the light of the affinities between them.

Secondly, consciousness is generally presupposed by the other mental phenomena we shall be discussing. So the problem of consciousness infects these other problems, spreading its intractability upon them, and giving them their special character. Those philosophers, then, who sense a scintilla of truth in my approach to consciousness (not those of the previous paragraph) may find their sympathies widening into other domains. The mind–body problem will be seen as not just a paradigm but a pervasive presence. In any case, it is the whole family of problems that needs to be treated, not each member in isolation.

NOTES

1 Perhaps we need a further distinction, which I shall mention but not pursue here – that between a puzzle and a mystery. It appears that we sometimes possess adequate theories that contain puzzling elements, as (say) with Newtonian theory and gravitation; this type of case is unlike that in which the domain of interest is deeply resistant to adequate theorizing, as (say) with consciousness. In the former type of case our cognitive capacities permit us to formulate the relevant theories but we cannot expel all sense of puzzlement about how the world is working; while in the latter type of case we cannot so much as formulate an explanatory theory that might contain puzzling pockets. TN can, in principle, be defined so as to admit both sorts of epistemic occlusion – localized puzzles and thoroughgoing mystery – but we shall be concerned with the second of these in this book (not that the distinction is obvious in every case). (I am indebted here to some suggestions of Chomsky made in correspondence.)

2 See Brian Farrell, 'Experience', and Thomas Nagel, 'What is it Like to be a Bat?'.

3 I have always taken this to be obvious, but confusion on the point is perhaps sufficiently prevalent to warrant some spelling out.

4   Similarly, the subjectivity of the human visual sense consists in the secondary qualities associated with that sense – *viz*. colours – and not in the way visual experiences strike our faculty of introspection, since the experiences would still possess subjective character even if we had no such higher-order faculty. The subjectivity of perceptual experience is a matter of how the *world* is perceived. See my *The Subjective View* for more on this.

5   It might be asked why consciousness is more problematic than magnetism or gravitation – these also being properties of matter that are puzzling to common sense. Part of the answer is that consciousness is an emergent or supervenient phenomenon, so that some bottom-up account ought to be possible of how it is produced; another part of the answer is that conscious states play no explanatory role in our developed theories of the material world, unlike magnetism and gravity. No doubt matter has its puzzling properties, but consciousness introduces a whole new dimension of puzzlement to that which exists independently of it. That is why dualism is a natural response to the fact of consciousness, as it is not for other properties of matter that may perplex us.

6   For a representative collection of essays, see Ned Block, *Readings in the Philosophy of Psychology*.

7   On consciousness as second-order belief, see David Rosenthal, 'Two Concepts of Consciousness'. The idea of criterionless self-ascription as definitive of a conscious state is a kind of Wittgensteinian version of essentially the same conception.

8   See John Searle, *The Rediscovery of the Mind*.

9   See Saul Kripke, *Naming and Necessity*.

10   See Wilfred Sellars, 'Empiricism and the Philosophy of Mind'.

11   See Ned Block, 'Troubles with Functionalism'.

12   See Donald Davidson, 'Mental Events', for a version of this approach.

13   If a straight irreducibility thesis were true in this case, then there should be no felt mind–body problem: the brain's possession of conscious properties ought to be no more puzzling than the fact that physical objects can have both shape and weight, each of these properties being irreducible to the other. But the existence and salience of the mind–body problem is a measure of the inadequacy of this kind of model. How *could* the brain have both material and mental properties? And in virtue of what do the latter properties depend upon the former?

14   Aphorism: 'the supernatural is human ignorance reified'.

15   Thus we had eliminative behaviourism at the beginning of the twentieth century and we have eliminative materialism toward its

end: see Paul Churchland, 'Eliminative Materialism and Propositional Attitudes'. Like most brands of optimism eliminativism takes
the form of denial.

16 But remember that incapacity in one domain is the natural upshot
of fluency in others: see Chomsky, *Language and Problems of
Knowledge*, chapter 5. A cut diamond will fail to reflect light in
certain directions – but only because it glitters impressively in others.

17 I should note that in that work I was more inclined to view the
mind–body problem as uniquely subject to TN; subsequent reflection, as reported in the present work, has convinced me that TN
has broader philosophical application than I at first thought.

18 Quoted in William James, *Principles of Psychology*, volume 1, p.
147.

19 See my, 'The Hidden Structure of Consciousness'.

3
Self

I The Problem: Persons and their Attributes

In the previous chapter we discussed conscious states; now we turn to the entities that bear such states – conscious subjects. The connection here is constitutive, since nothing counts as a person unless it is a bearer of consciousness; remove consciousness and you create a robot. Persons are to be *defined* as subjects of sensation, feeling, thought: I *am* the thing that enjoys such states of consciousness. It may not be a necessary condition of selfhood that one has the capacity for *reflective* consciousness – thoughts about one's first-order states of consciousness – but it is required that one have the states such thoughts concern *if* they are present. Indeed, the topic of the self is barely distinguishable from the topic of consciousness, in view of the intimacy of their relation; and the lie of the philosophical land is strikingly similar in the two cases. Accordingly, what we earlier said about consciousness is going to go over (with some reformulation) to the self. The self can be conceived as that which confers unity on conscious states, that which distinguishes one *centre* of consciousness from another; and the question then is the nature of this unifying principle. What makes my conscious states mine and yours yours?

The philosophical problem of the self consists in the fact that this question is extremely hard to answer. We cannot say what selves *are*. None of the obvious (or unobvious) candidates seems to have the properties we demand of the self. It can start to look as if selves belong to pseudo-ontology, along with all the other nonexistent beings. Commonsense psychology certainly works with an ontology of selves, which are constantly referred to, quantified over, and otherwise entified. We suppose that at any given time there exists a definite totality of them (though there may be borderline cases); that they come into and go out of existence; that they are fundamentally distinct from each other; that they change over time without ceasing to be; that they are objects of supreme moral worth; that they have mental and bodily characteristics. Thus we unreflectively assume, probably on the basis of our innate mental endowment, that persons constitute a set of well-individuated entities, as palpably real as anything else whose existence we accept. Yet philosophical reflection on this putative ontology rapidly turns vertiginous: we suffer from that peculiar philosophical anxiety which insinuates that, upon examination, *we don't know what we are talking about.*

Much has been written on personal identity over the years, and the subject has reached a high level of technical sophistication;[1] but I want to return, to begin with, to some basic intuitions and questions. What is the ultimate source of our perplexity here? Why are selves so ontologically problematic, in ways that material objects (say) are not? Part of the answer, surely, is that the referent of 'I' does not stand forth as a discrete entity in some object-containing medium such as space. Spatial occupancy is not, on the face of it, the mode of individuation proper to persons, at least primarily. Material objects (including human bodies) are located in space, taking up a certain volume of it and standing in measurable spatial relations to each other, and their distinctness plausibly consists in their spatial distribution. We can actually *see* that they are distinct, and what their distinctness depends upon, because perception reveals a plurality of objects disposed in space. Thus the individuation of material objects is (more or less) a perceptual given, perception being geared to the spatial. But, on the face of it, selves are not like that: the closeness of their connexion to consciousness removes them from the realm of simple spatial occupancy. The relation of selves to space thus becomes philosophically problematic. True, their bodies occupy space in the way other material objects do, but the self appears to be more than merely the body, considered as a physical object. The *I* of the *Cogito* is not just one material object among others. This is why our conception of the distinctness of persons cannot be tied directly to our perceptual apprehension of them. We have no sensory faculty relative to which selves are (immediately) presented as individuated one from another. I can see that your body is distinct from his, but I cannot in this way see that *you* are distinct from him, since selves are not perceptually presented in the way bodies are (though they may be perceptible in some derivative way). Therefore spatial individuation, backed by perceptual apprehension, is not, straightforwardly at least, available for the ontology of persons; indeed, for some philosophers, space and selves are worlds apart.[2] And so our favoured way of grounding and articulating acceptance of some range of entities has at best problematic application in the case of selves. Hence the ontological flailing that surrounds the topic.

And there is a second source of ontic elusiveness, equally familiar from the history of thought on the subject of the subject: the systematic transcendence of the self in acts of self-awareness.[3] If I try to focus on myself, making the referent of 'I' the object of my apprehension, then the subject of this focus inevitably transcends its object. When I think of myself that which thinks occurs as subject; thus I never become merely an object of my own apprehension. The self always, and systematically, steps out of cognitive reach. Even if the reflecting self and the self reflected upon are numerically identical, I can never stand back and apprehend this identity, since I shall always occur as a subject in my reflections as well as an object. *Qua* subject I can never be an intentional object to myself. Yet it is *qua* subject that I have my essence. This systematic elusiveness of the self makes it frustratingly difficult to pin down; we can get no cognitive fix on it. And there seems no guarantee that the self-as-subject retains its essential properties when we, as we say, consider ourselves as objects. Perhaps, indeed, the so-called self-as-object is really just some subset of the attributes of the self-as-subject – say, one's present state of consciousness. In any case, the subject stands aloof, tauntingly removed from the encounterable world.[4] No wonder our conception of it is apt to be so insubstantial, so blankly formal.

Pursuing such reflections, the self can seem at one moment to be the most indubitable thing in the world, with solipsism the only sure ontology, while a moment later it strikes one as the most incognizable of entities, a mere shadow of the grammar of 'I'. The philosophical problem is essentially that of securing our instinctive ontology of selves in the face of their inscrutability. In other words, we seek a theory of what selves *are* that is both intelligible and recognizably a theory of *selves*. This will naturally involve us in questions about the relationship between selves and their attributes – their bodies and minds. We need a theory of the nature of the self that links selves in the right way to their bodily and mental characteristics.

II DIME and the Self

The preceding remarks are an attempt to encapsulate, as nakedly as possible, the shape of the problem of the self as it naively appears, minimizing tendentious assumptions. I now want to set out the kinds of response to the problem that have suggested themselves to philosophers and others. Predictably, these responses have tended to condition the way the problem is conceived and formulated: the problem is apt to be approached with the specific solution to be offered in mind – at the cost, frequently, of over-looking key aspects of our notion of self. This needs to be borne in mind while surveying the self DIME.

Domesticating positions have been much favoured in the modern period, prompted largely by Hume's sceptical treatment of the subject, and recent analytic philosophy has tended to follow this path. The basic thought here is that self identity is not *sui generis*, that selves are not entities set radically apart from other entities with which they are associated; the self is explicable in terms of other, more familiar materials, which serve to remove the elusiveness and mystery that seem to belong to the self. It may be tempting to think that the self is a kind of perpetually receding dimensionless point, its essence untainted by anything more palpable, but actually, upon examination, we see that it is really nothing more than such and such facts in a misleading guise. This type of approach is thus aptly labelled reductive.[5] It may also be styled naturalistic, in the sense that it attempts to construct the self from resources whose naturalistic status (relatively speaking) has already been admitted. The self turns out to be less of an ontological embarrassment than we might have feared.

There are two main traditions of domesticating thought about the self. One tradition regards the self as nothing over and above the body: the referent of 'I' is simply the corporeal organism out of whose mouth the word issues. This tradition splits into a number of sub-theories, some emphasizing third-person bodily criteria of personal identity over time, others stressing the biological kind to which (human) persons belong, yet others stemming from a broader materialist metaphysics.[6] One variant picks on a particular part of the body as specially involved in self identity – the brain, naturally – and holds that our reference to selves is really a reference to this part of their bodies.[7] According to all these theories, the self is just one kind of physical object among others, its unity consisting in bodily unity, its essence reducing to that of the favoured parcel of matter. There are not physical organisms *and then* persons; rather, talk of persons is a fancy way of talking about the organisms whose place in our ontology has already been assured. Selves are thus not the exotic objects of some philosophers' wild imaginings.

The second domesticating tradition retains the mentalistic conception of the self but explains self identity in terms of certain psychological conditions.[8] The unity of the self over time or at a time consists in certain relations that hold between the mental attributes of selves. What makes a series of mental states the states of a single person is the fact that those states are related by such things as memory, causal continuity, psychological similarity and so forth. There is not some mysterious mental substance that *underlies* these relations and which constitutes the self; self identity is nothing more than the obtaining of these relations. Persistence, then, is the continued holding of the psychological relations that ground our talk of persons. To speak of a subject of consciousness is really to advert to these relations; anything else is just mystifying reification. The self is thus as empirically accessible as the contents of consciousness.

One can certainly appreciate the motivation for such theories: they offer to release us from the discomfort of finding the self to be the centre of one's world and yet oddly removed from it. They paint the self in colours we can recognize, reducing it to facts on which we have a better cognitive grip. In effect, they locate selves, respectively, within the world of perceived material objects or that of introspected mental items. And this provides us with a way of conceptualizing the ontology of selves: we can apply our concepts of the physical or the mental to the problematic entities, so bringing them within the scope of things we understand (comparatively speaking). To domesticate is to assimilate – to areas of our conceptual scheme with which we are more at home, from a theoretical point of view. We derive epistemic solace from such assimilations.

However, though D approaches are intelligibly motivated, it cannot be said that they have met with notable success. Like many reductive enterprises, they encounter serious obstacles. Without reviewing in detail the contemporary state of the subject, let me just record my conviction that none of the D theories that have been proposed holds water. There are systematic analytic problems of necessity, sufficiency and circularity; counterexamples to any proposal are readily produced; and there are still widely varying views about what a theory of personal identity should look like. In fact, the area resembles in these respects the state of debate over the mind–body problem. The self has not tamely submitted to theoretical domestication.[9]

Acknowledging the futility of D programmes, it is tempting to relax into irreducibility, suppressing one's explanatory urges. We should openly confess that the concept of a person is primitive, that there are no informative identity criteria to be given for persons, that persons are what they are and are not some other thing.[10] It is merely misplaced reductionism to balk at such primitiveness. Some things have to be taken as ontologically basic, intelligible only in their own terms, so why not say that selves are? True enough, there is no entity without identity – no category of genuine objects that fails to exhibit numerical sameness and difference – but it does not follow that every type of entity has nontrivial identity *conditions* – noncircular criteria of individuation. We can judge of the identity of persons well enough, and that should satisfy us. The only reply to the question 'what is a person?' is the trivial one: 'a person is a *person*'.

It is sometimes complained that I theses are uninformative. That is true, more or less, but it is not a good objection. The whole point of an I thesis is precisely that there *is* no informative account to be given – that is simply the way things are. It may make the world a less interesting place, but the world is under no obligation to be interesting. A better objection, which I shall develop after finishing my survey of the self DIME, is that there are certain facts that need to be *explained* about the self, and a blank I thesis leaves these dangling. There are, in particular, certain links between the self and other things that preclude a brute I thesis. For now let us simply note that I theses are plausible in proportion as what they concern is *independent* of what holds elsewhere in the world: so we shall need to ask whether selves have the kind of ontological independence or autonomy they must have in order to warrant an I thesis.

M doctrines have conspicuously thrived around the topic of self. Not uncommonly, selves have been thought capable of trans-migration, metempsychosis, reincarnation, exorcism, immortality, momentary departures from the body.[11] Supernaturalism comes naturally to selves; for they are not as other things. Often the self is conceived as the entity to which an explicitly religious meta-physics is primarily attached. And even if none of this is literally credited, the imagination is readily led in the direction of these ideas – as witness imaginative literature and psychoanalysis. The self is the fantasy object *par excellence*. It is tied to nothing, quite free-standing, and capable of contra-natural feats. Needless to say, radical dualism often lies behind these doctrines, standardly backed by a divine genesis story: the self must be immaterial, tenuously linked to the body, and God must have been its cause. Such an entity will not yield to prosaic domestication, and its irreducibility has a deep metaphysical explanation – it belongs to a separate unearthly world. Only the blind and impious could fail to grasp the numinous character of the self.

We serious scientific thinkers are not inclined to believe any of that: it is the product of a superstitious mentality that should have been put behind us long ago. Some of us even doubt whether such talk is meaningful, that it describes a genuine possibility. Nevertheless, as philosophers of the self, we should regard such excesses as data for reflection; for they tell us something signifi-cant about the concept of the self we have and how it sits in our conceptual scheme. It is, evidently, a concept that easily provokes extravagant and vapid speculation. There is something radically unanchored about the concept; it suffers from a kind of theoretical isolation, a lack of mesh with other concepts. Being thus unhinged, it falls prey to frictionless speculation – a sure symptom of epistemic transcendence. We are tempted by supernaturalism about the self because there is so little we can say of a soberly naturalistic kind about it. We have no fix on its objective essence; there is reference to the self without an accompanying theory of it. Thus fantasy flourishes around the concept.

Having reached this point, E conclusions promise a way out. If selves cannot be rendered mundane, and they are not simply brute existences, and they had better not be magical, then perhaps they are really nothing at all. Selves do not exist. *I* do not exist – nor do you. This is a part of the ontology of folk psychology that needs to be roundly repudiated. Conscious states there may be, but there are not *subjects* of consciousness – not really. We can admit animal organisms and their brains and their mental modules, but none of these adds up to a person, in our ordinary sense. We should conduct our neuroscience and psychology and ethics without including an ontology of persons, since no sense can be made of it. Selves should be sent the way of witches.

And yet, of course, this eliminative conclusion is hard to accept, here as in other areas. Can it really be literally true that *I do not exist*? Is my use of 'I' invariably empty of reference, so that nothing I say in the first person is ever true (or even false)? Am I to be prevented from saying how many people were in this room an hour ago? Must I give up the idea that my mental states are states of a person? This is strong medicine indeed. Surely the ontology of persons is rooted deep in our thought and speech; to abandon it would be to abandon something pervasive and useful, to say the least. We would need very strong reason indeed to contemplate such a large and drastic conceptual revision. If there is a defensible way of avoiding eliminating the self, then we should look to it with considerable sympathy.[12] TN is just such a way: it enables us to retain the self without commitment to any of the other unsatisfactory positions on the DIME shape. So let us consider its prospects.

III TN and the Self

We will not be surprised if TN about the subject of consciousness closely mirrors TN about consciousness itself. The key consideration here concerns the relationship between the self and the body: explaining this will force us to credit the self with properties that are not to be found represented in our given conceptual scheme. But before I get onto this I shall situate TN in relation to the self DIME and indicate how the CALM format fails to yield an intelligible account of how the self relates to its attributes.

First, TN offers a new and neglected point in logical space that needs to be reckoned with: it says that the self is an undomesticatable yet real entity that is neither inherently irreducible nor miraculous. Persons have properties that transcend our conceptual resources, and these properties are what make persons naturally possible. In view of this further option, then, it is a *non sequitur* to infer an E conclusion from the agreed failure of the DIM positions: that would be, in effect, to derive an ontological conclusion from merely epistemological premises. Human inexplicability never implies objective nonexistence: our inability to give an explanatory or reductive account of the self is a fact about our epistemology, not a reason to jettison that which resists our cognitive efforts; for we cannot assume that the true objective nature of the self is adapted to our given modes of cognition. And this point already undermines many of the standard moves that are made in discussions of the self, particularly those of a sceptical turn.[13]

In fact, in the light of the unattractiveness of the DIME positions, TN begins to look like the least unpalatable position to adopt, even if it could not be given any direct support. There are no sound objections of principle to it, while there are to the various DIME philosophies; it comports well with a general naturalistic perspective on the epistemology of the human knower; and the evidence from the course of debate on the subject of the self is entirely consonant with the truth of the TN hypothesis. Nor could the lack of direct support for TN count against its truth, since TN *entails* that it should not admit of direct support. To show directly that a certain problem is insoluble by a certain type of mind we need to be able to compare the actual solution to the powers possessed by that mind, so that we can demonstrate that the powers are not equal to the problem. We can provide this kind of demonstration when we ourselves have the solution to hand, as when we establish cognitive closure results for animals and children. But when the closure claim concerns ourselves this is obviously not feasible; only indirect support will be possible in such a case. It is quite possible, indeed, that TN be true of us with respect to a certain domain and yet this fact be unknowable *tout court* by us. At any rate, TN is clearly not refuted by the fact that it cannot be directly proved; given the form of the hypothesis, such unprovability is only to be expected. So TN is defensibly motivated and suffers no internal flaw. It also explains *why* the self DIME exists and is ultimately so unsatisfactory. Thus TN about the self needs to be taken seriously as a viable option.

The problem of the self could be put this way: what is the exact relation between the self and its attributes, both bodily and psychological? There we have the body, spatially extended, divisible into parts, a physical object among others; and there is the mind, the collection of mental states that 'belong' to the person – how do these things relate to the self who 'has' them? And the basic problem, as CALM predicts, is that no combinatorial story looks workable. The self has not the part–whole structure of the body, and is not divisible as the body is; so we cannot conceive of it as something of the order of the (mereological) sum of bodily components, as somehow intelligibly composed of what composes the body. Paradox results from the attempt to force the self into this mould, as when we insist on regarding the cerebral hemispheres (say) as literally two detachable and recombinable *parts* of the self. Similarly, classical empiricist views of the self as simply the totality of one's mental states, at a time and over time, run into familiar problems, notably in providing a criterion for the co-personality of pairs of mental states.[14] This suggests that the mistake is to try to construct the self, CALM-wise, from the mental states that, as we say, belong to it. The self is not *made of* its mental states: this is not the right relation to invoke here. Selves somehow transcend their mental states – they are not reducible to these states – and this is not capturable in CALM terms. 'Bundle theories' of the self, physical or mental, have CALM intentions, albeit subliminally so, but their general inadequacy suggests that CALM is the wrong format to adopt here. Thus the relation we indicate by saying that a person *has* both bodily and mental attributes is not explicable along CALM lines. That relation is not like the relation between a physical object and its constituents or the relation between a sentence and its constituents. It is altogether more mysterious and unique than that – hence the existence of a philosophical problem.

It is more than usually tempting at this point to declare the self and its relations irreducible and *sui generis*: there just is nothing illuminating to be said about what kind of thing the self is and its possession of mental and bodily attributes. The only constitutive properties the self has are those already recorded in our ordinary talk about selves, and we should rest content with that. But this quietist position is unsatisfactory because there exist certain kinds of dependence between selves and other things, and these require explanation. In the first place, persons are an emergent type of entity: it is only when organisms meet certain conditions, apparently of a biological nature, that they come to qualify as persons. This holds both phylogenetically and ontogenically: at some stage of evolution and individual growth organisms pass into the person category. But then there must be something that triggers this ontological transition, something about the organism that makes it possible and actual (compare consciousness). Presumably some brain property plays a critical part in this: I am a person while a tadpole is not because of some difference in our nervous systems. It is highly likely that organisms are destined for personhood (or not) by their genetic programme, so the genes must encode instructions for generating selves from living tissue. Thus there have to be principles that link selves to the materials that go into their production. Our *concept* of a person may be analytically primitive, but the things themselves need some kind of intrinsic natural architecture and mode of construction. Selves do not come from nowhere according to no natural process – they are biological products, like hearts and kidneys and conscious states.[15] Some natural science must be applicable to them, whether or not we can know its laws and mechanisms. It will not do, then, to declare selves and their properties inherently inexplicable, simply brute natural irreducibles.

Secondly, selves are subject to a kind of physical supervenience. If two bodies are physically identical (molecular duplicates) and one of them is a person, then so must the other be: no variation in personhood without some underlying physical variation. Similarly, if two brains are physically identical at a given time, and both are associated with persons, and if one brain undergoes physical changes that preserve the existence of its person, then it must also be the case that identical changes in the other brain will ensure the preservation of its person too. Personal identity over time is thus supervenient upon underlying physical facts: what keeps me in existence are certain physical conditions in my body, and you will be kept in existence too (necessarily so) if you duplicate those bodily conditions (given identical initial conditions). This is the analogue for persons of more familiar supervenience claims concerning mental states, and shares their motivation.[16] But now, such supervenience cannot be a mere accident: there has to be some explanation for why selves have this kind of dependence. In virtue of what does it obtain? What is it about selves and their bodies that makes them mesh together in these ways? For there is no ontological dependence without ontological explanation: resultants must be related thus-and-so to that from which they result.

TN accepts the need for underlying system in the heirarchy of supervenience, generally and in this special case, but it questions whether this system is humanly formulable. It conjectures that the blankness that attends our contemplation of these dependencies is principled and irremediable. More generally, it takes seriously the hypothesis that our perplexity about persons is the result of cognitive limits we cannot surmount. Our ontology of persons could only be made properly transparent if we could supply a level of explanation that systematically eludes us. TN says, first, that radical conceptual enrichment would be necessary to resolve our perplexities about the self; but, second, that the necessary enrichment exceeds what our cognitive apparatus permits (the first claim is obviously logically independent of the second). Objectively, selves slot smoothly into the natural biological world, according to natural principles; but our concepts fail to reveal how this comes about. And that is why the self is a subject of distinctively philosophical inquiry.

What form should TN take with respect to the self – how should it picture our ignorance? Following the lead set by our discussion of consciousness, a natural thought is that we need to invoke the idea of a hidden structure to the self.[17] In addition to the manifest aspects presented to introspection and observation, the self harbours an inner architecture that defines its unity and enables it to relate constructively to its physical basis in the body. According to TN, this hidden nature corresponds to nothing in our current conceptual scheme, even as a faint glimmer; so it is not, say, just the brain or some integrative property of it (at least as these are conceived by us). We lack the conceptual equipment needed to represent the objective essence of the self. Beings of other cognitive endowments might by contrast be able to grasp this essence, thus making science out of what for us languishes as perennial philosophy. Our epistemic relation to the self is like a monkey's relation to the physical world – apprehension without theoretical understanding. It is not that there is nothing more to the self than the attributes we ordinarily assign to it and the puzzle is how an entity so constituted could relate to body and mind; rather, the puzzle concerns what the self intrinsically *is* – its 'internal constitution'. But since we have no notion of what this might be like we are inclined to suppose that selves are exhausted by the appearances they present to our faculties. The idea of hidden structure goes against that pardonable (though fallacious) inclination. The self must have the richness of inner structure that the body has, without sharing that very structure. Just as it would be an idealist mistake to think that the body has no more structure than what is apparent to our ordinary perception of it, so it would be idealism about the self to think that *it* lacks properties beyond those accessible to our usual modes of access to it. For there is no guarantee that the requisite theory is available from the standpoint provided by these ordinary human modes of apprehension.

Of course, it goes against the grain to think that the self might harbour this kind of complex hidden constitution – for it strikes us as a simple nugget-like entity – but TN makes this counterintuitive claim intelligible: it results from the extreme epistemic gap that separates our conceptions from the objective nature of what they refer to. When you have no inkling of what the complexity of some entity might consist in you are naturally inclined to suppose that it is intrinsically simple – you tend to assimilate the nature of the entity to the appearances it presents to you. But

TN, combined with the idea of hidden structure, invites us to withstand this tendency in the case of the self: theory requires that we credit the self with much more than it reveals to us. The elusiveness of the self, already remarked upon, certainly suggests that our faculties for apprehending it fall woefully short of the mark – we can scarcely get it in our cognitive sights at all. It should really not amaze us, then, that our conceptual scheme provides us with such an impoverished tool for understanding this sector of its ontology. And this is what, for TN, brings philosophy into existence: reference accompanied by cognitive maladaptation. The reason the self is a philosophical topic but the body is not (at least in the same way) is that we are cognitively adapted to understanding bodies but we have no such natural adaptation in respect of the self (the predominant spatiality of our modes of conception plays a part in this). Converse intellectual adaptations would thus yield opposite classifications of these two topics of enquiry.

I shall end this chapter with a remark about death. The cessation of a person presumably consists in some change undergone by the person as a result of some efficient cause. Now suppose that selves have a substantial transcendent nature. Then the changes in them wrought at the point of death are likely to involve this nature. Thus these changes will occur in that region of the self to which we have no access. Therefore, there is a clear sense in which we do not know what our death will consist in: we do not grasp what it *is* for a self to go out of existence. (The same point could be made about birth – the onset of a self.) And this will naturally produce in us a sense of mystery about death. While we have a tolerable understanding of what it is for a body to cease to be alive, we are in the dark about what it is for the subject of consciousness to expire. We don't really know what we are being asked to envisage, beyond the simple fact of non-existence; the process itself is enigmatic. This sense of mystery is then apt to fuel our fear of death: the uncertainty augments the badness of sheer cessation. So the transcendent nature of persons shapes our attitude towards death, making it seem spookier than it objectively must be. On the other hand, perhaps if we could grasp what death deeply involves it might seem even more catastrophic than it does under our present conceptual scheme. Maybe we should be thankful that we cannot grasp our own nature.[18]

NOTES

1 For a collection of representative papers, see John Perry, *Personal Identity*; also Derek Parfit, *Reasons and Persons*.

2 Thus, notoriously, Descartes, who took selves to be essentially non-spatial, yet linked to a body whose essence is to be extended: to be a thinking being is necessarily not to be a spatial being.

3 See Jean-Paul Sartre, *The Transcendence of the Ego*.

4 Thus Wittgenstein: 'The philosophical self is not the human being, not the human body, or the human soul, with which psychology deals, but rather the metaphysical subject, the limit of the world – not a part of it.' *Tractatus Logico-Philosophicus*, 5.641.

5 As it is in Parfit, *Reasons and Persons*.

6 See Bernard Williams, *Problems of the Self*.

7 Thomas Nagel defends this position in *The View From Nowhere*, chapter 3.

8 This tradition extends from Hume's *A Treatise of Human Nature* to Parfit's *Reasons and Persons*. Russell characterizes it, aptly, as the view that a self is a series of classes of mental particulars, not a 'pin-point ego' that underlies the appearances: see his *Logic and Knowledge*, pp. 177–281.

9 I make a quick survey of some of the main problems in *The Character of Mind*, chapter 6.

10 On the primitiveness of persons, see P. F. Strawson, *Individuals*, chapter 3.

11 Consult most religions, and other sources of superstition.

12 We should distinguish the question of whether the ordinary concept of a person should be retained in a proper science of persons from the question of whether persons exist *tout court*. The concept *house* does not occur in the science appropriate to physical objects, including houses, but it does not follow – and is not true – that houses do not exist. I am concerned with eliminativism about the self in the stronger of these two senses, i.e. whether there are such things as persons; though I also believe that an ideal science of persons would contain a concept at least extensionally equivalent to our concept *person*. The point of TN is not to insist that our ordinary concepts occur in the ideal theory of the world, but rather to make room for the idea that this theory will reckon with the entities to which we commonsensically refer – conscious states, persons, meaning, acts of will, and so forth.

13 Of course, eliminativism is *consistent* with terminal cognitive intractability; the point is that it does not follow from that alone. We

need a reason to accept that the best explanation of the intractability is ontological in character – and this is what is typically lacking. Hence the eliminativist *non sequitur*.

14 Hume was already aware of this in the Appendix to the *Treatise*, where he declares himself at a loss to discover the principles that link successive or contemporaneous perceptions into a single self.

15 I do not mean to assert that selves are *necessarily* biological entities, merely that the ones we know about are. Whether there can be non-biological selves is one of those questions that requires access to a theory that eludes us – at least if we are to *understand* the basis of the possibility or impossibility in question. A parallel point holds for the other mental phenomena I discuss in this book.

16 On supervenience, see Jaegwon Kim, 'Psychophysical Supervenience'; also my, 'Philosophical Materialism'.

17 See my, 'The Hidden Structure of Consciousness'.

18 I suspect that the human readiness to believe in the natural possibility of immortality stems from TN about the self: if we could grasp the deep way in which the self depends upon the body, then we would not be inclined to believe that selves are essentially independent of bodily disintegration. The question of personal immortality would resemble that of whether a tree can survive being burnt to ashes.

4

Meaning

I The Problem: Thought and Its Objects

Selves, consciousness, meaning: a redoubtable philosophical tradition takes these categories to be inextricably intertwined. Selves are taken to be the original fount of meaning, and states of consciousness are its primary vehicle – intentionality is essentially the product of conscious subjects. But we do not need to agree with this strong three-way inextricability thesis in order to recognize the deep connections between these three topics. Whether the dependency relations here are conceptually necessary, they are certainly pronounced and prevalent. So we might reasonably expect that the human ability to mean things will present the same kind of recalcitrance that we have seen attends consciousness and personhood. Mysteries tend to come in clusters. We should anticipate a comparable order of difficulty in explaining what meaning is and what makes it possible. Our cognitive design inhibits us from understanding the nature of our semantic capacities, as it does those other two items. At any rate, this chapter will suggest that meaning also is apt for TN treatment.

While meaning things is an effortless achievement for most of us, it is extraordinarily difficult to command a clear view (as Wittgenstein puts it) of what this achievement involves, let alone answer the deep explanatory and constitutive questions the phenomenon of meaning raises. When I use the word 'red', or employ the concept *red* in thought, I mean something definite by it, referring to something in the world, and this is distinct from what I mean by other words and concepts. A certain portion of reality falls, as it were, within the semantic cone projected by my performance; a quite particular relation is somehow established between me and the distinguished portion. Something about me is responsible for establishing this relation, perhaps in conjunction with my situation in the world. What is the general nature of the relation thus established? What distinguishes my semantic relations to the world from the multitude of other relations I have to it? This is intended, initially, as a descriptive or phenomenological question, not an explanatory one: what phenomenon is it that we are trying to account for? It is a question about what we ordinarily mean by 'meaning', about its pretheoretical character. For we need to have some workable handle on the *explanandum* before we can really broach the underlying how-possible explanatory questions; and, as with consciousness and the self, this is part of the philosophical problem – we have difficulty even saying articulately what it is that we find perplexing.[1]

Let me then begin by identifying three central features of our commonsense notion of meaning, with a view to formulating the essence of the philosophical problem. The first of these I shall call, for want of a better word, the *fertility* of meaning: the way in which even the simplest of words or concepts generates an enormous range of potential applications. Meaning is a remarkably inclusive or far-reaching phenomenon. Just consider 'red': its extension includes every last red object, past, present and future, as well as all counterfactually red objects; and hence the meaning of this little word determines indefinitely many uses of the word as correct or incorrect, according as the word is applied to members of its extension or otherwise. The vast majority of these objects have never been encountered by one who is master of the word's meaning, and the potential uses of the word go far beyond any that may be made in the speaker's lifetime. Yet on any single occasion of use the meaning of the word will include all these objects and constrain all these uses. It follows that there exists some property, instantiated by the speaker, in virtue of which he grasps this capacious yet exclusive meaning: his faculties must be capable of the feat of encompassment his meanings entail. Semantic mastery thus involves a kind of generality that relates the speaker to items that vastly exceed those with which he has had any kind of commerce.

This generality, which is both principled and fecund, is perhaps most striking with respect to mathematical terms, because such terms commonly introduce relations to strictly infinite totalities. Consider '+': this term denotes a certain binary function which, when applied to any of infinitely many pairs of numbers, yields a unique number as its value. Something about one's mastery of '+' implies that this infinitary object, and not some other one, is the referent of one's uses. But of course only a vanishingly small subset of the numbers to which addition may be applied have actually been added together by human beings. Nevertheless, we can pick out a unique function by '+', despite our paltry efforts at exhausting the number series by acts of addition. Our meanings thus transcend the finite character of our own semantic behaviour.[2] Intentionality has infinity built into it. And this property of meaning is not some marginal aberration, confined to a specialized vocabulary; it is part of the general nature of meaning. The whole point of meaning, we might say, is to enable thought to exceed the bounds of acquaintance: it can take us any distance in any direction, travelling across arbitrarily extensive portions of reality, yet keeping to fixed rails as it does so. That it can cope with the mathematical infinite is only to be expected, since size and remoteness are in general no obstacle to the inclusive powers of meaning. Meaning enables our thoughts to go where our bodies and senses could never take us – the past, the future, the merely possible, and so on.

A second characteristic of meaning – still speaking at the level of descriptive phenomenology now – is its curious impalpability. To employ a concept or mean something by a word is not to host some isolable element in the flux of mental events: meanings are not like pains and tickles and sudden emotions.[3] That one's state of mind represents some particular external state of affairs is not a discriminable component in what passes before one's consciousness; nor is it a perceptible feature of one's outward appearance. Somewhat like the self, meaning has a certain elusiveness, and not because it is too small or distant: what I mean by my words is not set out for me in a containing medium within which individual items are arrayed for my inspection. This is why there is a serious question as to the nature of one's knowledge of one's own meanings: no model of how this knowledge works suggests itself. It is natural, then, to conclude that there is nothing for meaning to consist in or of; it does not appear to *be* anything in particular.[4] It is oddly diaphanous, wraithlike, like a cloudy presence surrounding a word. The quintessentially philosophical question, 'what *is* it?', is readily evoked by meaning. And, as the preceding remarks show, it attracts unsatisfactory metaphors in an attempt to capture one's intuitions about the kind of being it is. The impalpability of meaning makes it hard to put one's descriptive finger on it. Moreover, this kind of unlocatability seems bound up with the inclusiveness and fertility of meaning: only something thus diffuse and unhemmed could succeed in reaching beyond the concrete particulars of the specific occasion of semantic performance; meaning can take so much in because it is not itself tied down to any chunk or stretch of space and time (note those jejune metaphors again). It can thus appear that meaning is both everywhere and nowhere at the same time. Meaning is precisely *not* like a beam of light radiating outward from the semantic subject.

Thirdly, the notion of meaning carries with it the notion of correctness: conditions of truth and falsity attach to the use of words, as well as justification and its opposite. There is no such thing as meaning something by a word and it being undetermined what counts as a correct utterance of the word. For a predicate to have an extension *is* for it to be fixed what counts as a correct application of that predicate: it applies correctly to all and only the members of its extension.[5] So any account of what constitutes meaning must respect these norms of correct use; it cannot leave open or indeterminate what is to count as meeting the conditions of correctness of a word's use.[6] Meaning is what permits the formation of true or false utterances, and what constitutes it must therefore yield linguistic norms that conform to the meaning of the term in question. We must so represent meanings that correctness conditions emerge as *internal* to their nature, as direct consequences of the kind of thing they are. In short, meaning must not lose its connection with truth. A condition of the possibility of meaning, therefore, is that truth-requirements should attach determinately to strings of words or concepts. An adequate theory of meaning needs to ensure that meaning can have this essential property.

In keeping with the acronymic trend of this book, let me refer to these three features of meaning as the FIN-features. Then we can say that the philosophical task, as it initially presents itself anyway, is to give an account of meaning that preserves the FIN-features: we have to explain what meaning is in such a way that it has the fertility, impalpability and normativeness that we naively associate with meaning. Only thus will we have given a philosophical theory of meaning itself and not of some pale imposter for the real thing. And the philosophical difficulty is simply that no theory meeting these requirements looks feasible: nothing we can produce seems to add up to what we pretheoretically expect of meaning. Our folk semantics provides us with quite a rich set of semantic concepts, but it does not appear to contain the materials for a meta-theory of these concepts. It uses the idea of meaning, but it does not say what meaning *is*. In a way that is characteristic of philosophical perplexity, we find ourselves having to hunt around for theoretical resources with which to cobble together (always unsatisfactorily) what we had taken for granted. Our conceptual scheme is notably thin when it comes to providing a theory of its own pivotal notions; it is opaque to itself. This is the condition in which philosophical puzzlement typically arises – we confront a sudden deep impasse in trying to make sense of our familiar notions. Next, then, we must trace out the DIME shape as it applies to the case of meaning, noting its way with the FIN-features.

II DIME and Meaning

In the case of meaning the DIME shape is more than usually sharply delineated, perhaps because the subject has been so intensively considered in recent philosophy. It has become painfully clear what the options are; though, as I shall suggest, the TN option is systematically neglected, it being assumed that the theoretical nature of meaning *must* be transparent to semantic beings such as ourselves. Let me then rapidly and loftily survey the standard positions, just to locate them on the philosophical map.

Attempts to domesticate meaning have been many and various. Typically, the hopeful theorist endorses an identity claim with respect to meaning: to have a semantic attribute *is* to instantiate such and such a condition, where the condition is specified in terms not themselves overtly semantical. Thus semantic facts are brought under concepts with a wider application, drawn from elsewhere in our conceptual scheme, so showing that meaning has an intelligible and law-abiding nature. Meaning is possible because it is an instance of something more general, which is itself agreed to be (relatively) unproblematic. The FIN-features do not then, upon analysis, undermine the possibility of what they purport to characterize. We can divide D theories into two broad groups, corresponding to whether a first- or third-person standpoint is adopted. The first type of theory identifies meaning with supposed elements in the stream or field of consciousness – paradigmatically, mental images.[7] The thought is that these elements will successfully duplicate the properties of the meanings they underlie: in particular, they will determine the right set of items as the reference of the term in question, say by virtue of resemblance to the image. Commonly, such theories seek to reduce semantic representation to something more pictorial. They are the analogue, broadly speaking, of theories of the self that identify selves with introspectable contents of consciousness. The second type of theory eschews consciousness and its contents and locates meaning in more objective facts about the thinker or speaker. Some see causal or teleological or nomological relations to the environment as constitutive of meaning/reference.[8] Others see meaning as an essentially behavioural phenomenon, as a matter of dispositions to use, functional roles, procedures of verification or falsification.[9] Yet others prefer to locate meaning further inward, in neural architectures or processes of various kinds.[10] On these views, meaning is just matter under some kind of complex structural or functional description, where the description is formulable from within the framework of our thought. The domestication programme here follows that of other broadly materialist world views: matter in motion as the ideal of intelligibility.

A third approach declines to answer the constitutive question about meaning, sensing futility in that direction, and proposes instead to think of meaning as an essentially combinatorial phenomenon.[11] What we need to do in order to tame meaning is to show how simple semantic units combine to generate more complex ones according to stateable rules. The meaning of the basic elements is left uncommented upon, and the work goes into devising formal principles that yield the correct assignments to derived structures. The insight is to come from articulating compositional relations, not from confronting the question of what kind of thing meaning intrinsically is. Once the semantics of a language has been finitely axiomatized no further domestication is held to be required. Meaning is 'implicitly defined' by a theory of its combinatorial powers.

Semantic irreducibility theses reject explanatory or analytic efforts to secure semantic facts by way of non-semantic notions. Instead meaning is taken to be a primitive constituent of the world, with semantic terms as analytically basic as the fundamental terms of geometry.[12] Words and concepts are representationally related to the world, but no account can be given of what this relation consists in or depends upon. It simply is. There is nothing about a thinker in virtue of which his thoughts refer to things – save that they do so refer. Domestication is neither necessary nor possible. Only dogmatic ontological anti-pluralism could stand in the way of accepting meaning on its own terms, FIN-features and all. There is thus no legitimate cause for philosophical puzzlement about the place of the semantic in the wider world: it is just a plain fact about us that we mean things, as it is that we digest and kick them. Meaning belongs to the same rich and variegated realm as irreducible selves and inexplicable states of consciousness: we have here a veritable zoo of autonomous and primitive realities.

Magical conceptions of meaning have tended to be more subliminal than official, dangers not doctrines. Wittgenstein writes: 'we are most strongly tempted to imagine that giving a name consists in correlating in a peculiar and rather mysterious way a sound (or other sign) with something. How we make use of this peculiar correlation then seems to be almost a secondary matter. (One could almost imagine that naming was done by a peculiar sacramental act, and that this produced some magic relation between the name and the thing.)'[13] And it is, of course, a general theme of his that meaning provokes 'queer' and 'superlative' flights of fancy in us.[14] The beginning of St John's gospel might be read as sanctifying this idea with overt theology: 'In the beginning was

the Word, and the Word was with God, and the Word was God.'
Here the Word must presumably be construed semantically not
syntactically, so that the identity thesis propounded in the final
conjunct equates divinity with significance and not with mere
orthography (I do not intend this as serious biblical interpretation). According to this way of thinking, then, semantic relations
belong with spell-castings and telepathic relations – non-naturally
mediated archings out, obscurely suggestive of numinous realms.

More soberly, the Platonic metaphysics of meaning, in which
the world of abstract Forms is prenatally apprehended by the
discarnate soul, and a process of recollection is needed to recover
this acquaintance, certainly has the ring of the magical and mystical
about it.[15] We might also cite the mysticism of Wittgenstein's
Tractatus as hospitable to the magical imagery disavowed by his
later work, though the usual difficulties of interpretation should
be noted.[16] At any rate, assigning the picturing relation to the
domain of the unsayable clearly puts it beyond the world of
stateable fact; this is to give meaning an occult aroma, inviting us
to reserve a special parallel shadow world for it to inhabit,
glimpsed only obliquely.

Eliminative recommendations are apt to follow a survey of the
above options, and for the usual sorts of reason. If we cannot
manage to domesticate meaning, yet we balk at its irreducibility
and scorn semantic mysticism, then we have no alternative than
to expel it. Semantic nihilism or irrealism is our only resort. Thus
we have become familiar with such claims as that there is no fact
of the matter about what we mean, or that purely syntactic
descriptions of mental states must suffice, or that semantic attributions are merely instrumental, or that the whole idea of meaning
is so much 'loose talk' – all bold attempts to banish semantic
description from our considered view of the world.[17] For if there
is simply no such thing, then there can be no question of having
to give a satisfactory theory of it. The FIN-features, on this view,
effectively price meaning out of existence.

III TN and Meaning

Given the nature of the thesis, TN is never going to wear its truth
on its face for the cognitive beings to whom it applies, but there

are special reasons why TN about meaning should be the last position to occur to us – without, however, these reasons counting against the correctness of the thesis. We are naturally prone to assume that the full nature of meaning must be accessible to us, that the correct theory of it should fall within our representational powers. First, meaning and its correct theory are items of the same ontological type: a theory of meaning is a set of meanings (propositions), a representation of representation. We tend to assume that our representational powers are adequate to explain our representational powers. Of course, this is a mistake, as reflection on the intellectual predicament of thinking animals already suggests – but it is a tempting mistake nonetheless. Second, we enjoy a unique epistemic relation to our own meanings: we know what we mean with special authority, possibly greater than that of our knowledge of our own sensations and the like. This transparency of meaning to our first-person faculties of awareness is then apt to encourage the assumption that we are guaranteed to be in a position to develop the right theory of what we know so intimately. This too is a mistake, since we can know about something under one sort of description without being able to bring it under others. To gain the right perspective on the theoretical problems posed by meaning, untainted by the natural modes of access we have to it, we need to abstract away from our first-person awareness of what we mean, considering the FIN-features in a more objective fashion. We have to ask how any system composed as we are could come to instantiate properties with this set of defining features: then we can leave intellectual space for the idea that what we know so immediately might not be theoretically understandable by us.

Once TN about meaning has been formulated and shown not to be ruled out by any acknowledged fact about meaning, the usual DIME dialectic must be reconsidered. It will now be a clear *non sequitur* to infer eliminativism from the agreed inadequacies of the other three options; in particular, the inevitable failure of domesticating programmes might be interpretable, not as a demonstration of ontological disrepute, but as a reflection of the limitations of our theory-generating capacities, so that E positions are simply denying the existence of what is not intelligible to human cognition – a piece of straight idealism by the standards of TN. We are then at liberty to construe indeterminacy theses, according to which no (non-semantic) fact can be found that captures the semantic distinctions we naively make, as a *reductio* of the idea that all the facts relevant to constituting meaning are ascertainable by us. That a suitable fact cannot be *found* (by us) does not entail that there *is* no fact. It is not that meaning is objectively indeterminate but that what makes it determinate is not something that falls within our cognitive field of vision.[18] Putting it polemically, the possibility of TN here shows that a good deal of the standard argumentation about the reality of meaning rests upon an idealist fallacy. And perhaps the very rebarbativeness of indeterminacy theses and their ilk is a reason to view TN with favour.

The difficulty about meaning is essentially a difficulty about relating levels of description. The levels are evidently systematically related, but we cannot provide any satisfactory account of this relation. Structurally, then, the problem resembles the problem of consciousness. In the case of meaning, we have, on the one hand, a level of description in which properties with the FIN-features are ascribed and, on the other, a level in which these features seem notably absent – the description of the organism as a causal (though conscious) centre of reactions and dispositions. This latter description is finite, palpable and norm-free. The problem, then, is to find some way to bring these levels together. Simple identity theses fail to preserve the FIN-features, but no other story seems to provide a direct enough link. Thus, there must be some constitutive link between meaning and use, for example, but simply identifying meaning with occasions of use leads to notorious problems of principle.[19] The problem, here as elsewhere, can be conveniently stated in terms of supervenience. If two beings agree in all non-semantic descriptions – behavioural, inner and relational – then they must mean and think the same things; yet nothing in the supervenience base can capture the essential nature of semantic properties, as encapsulated by the FIN-features: so what then is the precise relation between the two levels? This is a problem of explanation, of rendering transparent and intelligible what is otherwise merely brute. *How* can meaning, constituted as it is, depend upon, emerge from, properties that cannot in themselves duplicate the powers of semantic properties? There is a gap in our understanding here. TN proposes to take this explanatory gap at face-value, not construing it in any of the ways prescribed by the DIME options. We simply lack the concepts requisite to joining the two levels together in a unified theory. We would need radically new concepts in order to deliver the absent explanatory framework. But, according to TN, this conceptual innovation lies beyond our given cognitive powers, in a sector of intellectual space we cannot reach.

How antecedently probable is TN about meaning? Let me begin by repeating an essential background principle whose importance cannot be exaggerated. We might call it 'the principle of cognitive specificity': any terrestrial (as opposed to divine) cognitive being exhibits areas of cognitive strength and cognitive weakness, depending ultimately on its biological endowment. The idea of 'general intelligence' makes no absolute sense, at least as a realistic empirical description of evolved organisms such as ourselves. So we know on general grounds that the human cognitive system, like that of other species, will have its cognitive specificities – its areas of smooth success, faltering progress, and sheer blindspots. Thus in evaluating the cognitive powers of a species we should take seriously the evidence for cognitive specificity that the species actually exhibits; tentatively, to be sure, as befits all empirical evidence, especially at such a high theoretical level, but nevertheless with the impartiality proper to the subject. Accordingly, systematic failure of intellectual effort in a certain domain, unaccompanied by an explanation in terms of objective properties of that domain, is *prima facie* evidence that here we have an instance of what the principle of cognitive specificity predicts on general grounds. Philosophical reflection on the nature of meaning is taken by TN to be a plausible candidate for an area of intellectual effort in which human cognitive specificities are not cut out for the task. The deep puzzlement and ultimate blankness we experience when trying to make the pieces fit together is a result of cognitive maladaptiveness with respect to questions of this general class. We are like rats trying to solve a type of maze whose configuration falls outside any of which they can form a cognitive map.[20] Certainly, it would be quite wrong for these hapless rats to conclude from their difficulty either that there is really no maze to be solved after all (E) or that it must somehow fall into the class of mazes they can solve if only they put more effort into redescribing it (D) or that they are in the presence of the divine maze-maker whose mazes partake of the mystical (M) or that there is simply nothing to be said about what constitutes a maze as of one kind rather then another (I). No, in this case (by stipulation) it is simply that their failed efforts to escape result from inherent limitations on their maze-representing abilities.

We should seriously consider, then, whether our own difficulties in escaping from the maze of meaning might result from architectural limits on our faculties. And to do this it helps to bear in mind what those faculties are *for*. Our epistemic faculties are, plainly, representational in character; so their job is to signify states of affairs. But what states of affairs? Well, originally and primarily, states of affairs germane to our well-being – those we *need* to represent in order to thrive. These include states of the physical world and mental states. Plausibly, then, we are genetically programmed to represent things of these specific kinds, this enabling us to adapt successfully to our environment with the minimum of cognitive effort. Most of what we are designed to represent therefore is non-semantic, with some simple semantics thrown in to help us exploit the other-negotiating power of folk psychology. But, given this teleological background, there is no good reason to assume that we should be equipped to grasp what makes meaning possible; for its underlying enabling principles are not of any interest to a faculty designed as ours is. Monkeys too, one assumes, exploit some primitive semantic notions in dealing with their conspecifics, but this biologically motivated capacity obviously does not extend to understanding the philosophy or science of the properties and relations so exploited: monkeys are constitutionally incapable (going by present evidence) of solving the theoretical problems about meaning that puzzle us humans, and indeed are blissfully unaware of these problems (one hopes!). Why assume, then, that their nearest biological relatives, *homo sapiens*, have suddenly acquired the kind of meta-capacity needed to understand how meaning arises from a world of meaningless goings on? My point is this: if we were equipped to understand our semantic capacities that would be a biological accident – and not one that is predictable from the point of view of what is non-accidental. There is thus every reason to expect what we apparently find: that our representational powers, while reasonably adept at taking in the workings of the external world, are notably impoverished when it comes to comprehending their own nature, leaving us philosophically perplexed about their basis and possibility. Meaning, after all, is not present in us in order to enable us to understand its own nature, but rather to stand for other things. TN sees significance in this fact.

How does CALM relate to meaning? Ambivalently but instructively, is the answer. On the one hand, the one aspect of meaning into which we seem to have real insight, namely its combinatorial properties, fits naturally into the CALM framework. The Fregean scheme of functional composition, variously refined and supplemented, which finds an isomorphism between syntactic and semantic complexity, nicely exemplifies a structure congenial to CALM comprehension. However, this style of theorizing encounters resistance when it comes to other aspects of meaning, especially the relation between meanings (simple or complex) and other properties of the semantic subject. The general nature of meaning, and its foundations, do not fit into the CALM mould. I suspect that the attraction, always hard to stifle, of interpretational views of what confers meaning, on which the meaning of a symbol is fixed by that of some other semantically privileged symbol, stems at least in part from adherence to CALM bias: we are tempted to see meaningfulness as consisting in a kind of quasi-syntactic concatenation between the symbol to be interpreted and a symbol that provides that interpretation.[21] Once this type of view is seen to be unworkable we are left with nothing CALM-like to rely upon. Invoking linguistic use, conceived as token utterances over time in distinctive situations, does not supply us with a CALM theory, since the relation between meaning and use in this sense is notoriously problematic. Certainly we cannot represent meaning as somehow the *sum* of such token uses, as their fusion, on pain of losing the FIN-features; so the relation between meaning and use does not fit the CALM format – meaning is not any kind of combination of occasions of use. Generally, the non-semantic phenomena in which meaning is manifested, or on which it depends, are not related CALM-wise to semantic properties. Hence the difficulty of articulating the relations in question: the FIN-features cannot be seen as CALM products of other traits and features of the semantic subject.

Of course, I am not claiming in any of this to have proved TN about meaning. I have certainly not refuted the many theories that exist which purport to answer the question of what makes meaning possible. Nor have I claimed that nothing whatever of interest can be said about the nature of meaning, that it is wholly epistemically transcendent. My intention has been to sketch an alternative position on the subject, one which is both neglected and plausible. This position, once identified, can serve to ease certain philosophical pressures, especially of an eliminativist kind, and render the frustrations of theory construction intelligible. Perhaps the best we can do, as theorists of meaning, is to duplicate or simulate certain structural properties of meaning in non-semantic terms, without ever really getting to the heart of the phenomenon itself.[22] For, to speak broadly, it is hard to see how we could ever produce a full theory of our semantic capacities without achieving a general understanding of mind.

IV Meaning and Will

I shall end this chapter by forging a link with the next one. The link will illustrate the point made in the final sentence of the previous section. It is common to hear it said that meaning will not become properly intelligible to us until consciousness does; what I want to suggest is that we cannot ultimately detach the study of meaning from that of the will, so that the puzzles raised by the latter attach also to the former. Unfortunately, this is often disguised by the terms in which meaning is discussed. Many theorists of meaning have discerned a necessary bond between what someone means and his or her behaviour, conceived in various ways: doing is integral to meaning.[23] And there does seem to be something right in this idea, hard as it may be to formulate with any precision; the volitional connotations of 'intentionality' are not inappropriate to the phenomenon. But this has an obvious consequence for the location of the meaning faculty in the overall economy of the mind, namely that it joins constitutively with the faculties responsible for action. In a word, meaning involves the faculty of will. Nor is the dependence asymmetric, since willing also requires meaning, i.e. mental states with representational content. But this interdependence implies that there can be no full account of the semantic faculties that remains silent about the volitional faculties, and vice versa. And this in turn implies that the distinctive properties of the will are bound up with the nature of meaning; in particular, that property of the will we call its *freedom* is connected to meaning. For the behaviour in which I typically manifest meaning is precisely a case of free action: that is indeed what human speech is. So free will is exercised in the expression of meaning, and this expression is integral to the nature of meaning. Meaning *is* that which I freely express in my linguistic and other acts (under a use-oriented conception of meaning): the nature of the one enters into the nature of the other.

A tight mystery cluster results from this overlapping of essences. On the one hand, the mystery of meaning attaches itself to the problem of the will, since the will works by intentionality (at least as conceived in folk psychology). Whatever view we take of meaning will thus have consequences for our view of the will. On the other hand, if willing is essential to meaning, then any mysteries that attend the volitional faculties will transfer to the semantic faculties. To be specific, the problem of freedom comes to haunt the philosophy of meaning.[24] As we shall see in the next chapter, this adds yet another large dimension of mystery to our understanding of what it is to mean something, since freedom is the philosophical mystery *par excellence*.

NOTES

1 Ordinary usage provides little guidance here, as witness the various senses of 'means'; hence philosophers and others introduce semi-technical terminology with which to pin their topic down ('sense', 'reference', 'extension' etc.). Our basic subject-matter here is, I take it, the capacity of an agent's conscious states to be about states of affairs of various kinds. But, of course, this characterization leaves many unanswered questions.

2 I am here relying upon Saul Kripke's discussion of '+' in *Wittgenstein on Rules and Private Language*.

3　See Wittgenstein, *Philosophical Investigations*; and my, *Wittgenstein on Meaning*.

4　Wittgenstein appears to embrace this idea: 'The mistake is to say that there is anything that meaning something consists in.' *Zettel*, section 16.

5　Of course, there is vagueness and 'open texture' in natural language; but still there are conditions of correct and incorrect use for such terms.

6　This point is emphasized in Kripke's *Wittgenstein on Rules and Private Language*.

7　Thus the British empiricists and their descendants.

8　The following are representative: Fred Dretske, *Knowledge and the Flow of Information*; Ruth Millikan, *Language, Thought and Other Biological Categories*; Jerry Fodor, *A Theory of Content and Other Essays*.

9　See W. V. Quine, *Word and Object*, and Michael Dummett, 'What is a Theory of Meaning?'

10　Connectionists of some varieties fall into this group: see J. McClelland and D. Rumelhart, *Parallel Distributed Processing: Explorations in the Microstructure of Cognition*.

11　See Donald Davidson, *Inquiries into Truth and Interpretation*.

12　Kripke suggests something like this in *Naming and Necessity*; I toyed with the idea in *Wittgenstein on Meaning*, chapter 4.

13　Wittgenstein, *The Blue and Brown Books*, p. 172.

14　See, for example, *Philosophical Investigations*, section 38.

15　Plato, *The Republic*.

16　Wittgenstein says: 'There are, indeed, things that cannot be put into words. They *make themselves manifest*. They are what is mystical.' *Tractatus*, 6.522.

17　Thus: Quine, *Word and Object*; Stephen Stich, *From Folk Psychology to Cognitive Science*; Daniel Dennett, *The Intentional Stance*.

18　I mean this as a reply to both Quine's indeterminacy thesis and Kripke's semantic sceptic.

19　See Wittgenstein *Philosophical Investigations*, section 138. Kripke brings out how problematic the relation is in *Wittgenstein on Rules and Private Language*.

20　This analogy was suggested to me by a remark of Chomsky made in correspondence.

21　Wittgenstein saw this as a standing temptation in reflection about meaning; the CALM conjecture explains why the temptation comes so naturally to us.

22   I am here distinguishing between giving a theory of the nature of meaning and providing a model (in the quasi-technical sense) of meaning. It may be, for example, that there is some kind of iso-morphism between the normative aspects of meaning and certain sorts of causal or nomic relations to the environment – as in Fodor's asymmetric dependence theory: see *A Theory of Content*. But it does not immediately follow that meaning can be *identified* with such relations, or reduced to them. For, first, the relations in question might hold only in virtue of prior semantic facts, and hence be derivative from meaning not constitutive of it. And, second, a structural mapping is not the same as a theory: it is merely to find a relation of correspondence between two sorts of fact. I am re-minded of attempts to explain self-consciousness as consisting simply in an auto-scanning mechanism: there is, indeed, a structural analogy here, but it does not add up to a genuine theory of the nature of self-consciousness. To simulate certain aspects of a phenomenon is not *ipso facto* to characterize the real nature of that phenomenon. I suspect that a good deal of pseudo-illumination with respect to the mind comes from conflating theories with analogies. According to TN, however, analogies – more or less partial and unsatisfactory – are all we can realistically expect.

23   Quine and Wittgenstein are obvious examples.

24   This consequence is typically obscured by mechanistic talk of 'outputs' and 'functional roles' and 'dispositions': but it is clear upon examination that episodes of free will are being tacitly invoked. Linguistic use is, indeed, a paradigm instance of free human action.

5

Free Will

I The Problem: Freedom and the Causal Order

The problem of freedom is that the concept can appear to impose requirements that cannot be reconciled with any available conception of how the world works. No matter how we conceive of the course of events we cannot find room for the idea of a free choice. Thus the concept strikes us, upon reflection, as inherently paradoxical. The question is whether we can resolve the apparent paradox and preserve the possibility of freedom. In this chapter I shall ask whether TN can play a part in this salvage effort. Does our perplexity result from deep ignorance about the real nature of free choice? Are we, indeed, compelled, by the modes of thought natural to us, to conceive of freedom in ways that are ill-suited to its true character, forcing it into a conceptual framework that (misleadingly) compromises its objective reality?

The topic of free will is connected to our previous three topics. Only conscious beings are capable of acting freely; though the ground of this necessary condition is far from clear. The agent of free choice is evidently the self; though the relation between self and choice is unperspicuous. And the operations of will have meaning or intentional content; though what determines this is obscure. A free decision is a conscious event, on the part of a person, bearing semantic properties. Thus it is surrounded on all sides by theoretical recalcitrance, as well as carrying troubles peculiar to itself. It lies at the dead centre of what perplexes us.

Despite the puzzles free will presents, however, it is deeply embedded in our ordinary intuitive folk psychology. All human interaction, and self-reflection, is suffused with the idea of freedom; there is nothing marginal or exceptional about it. Freedom is a property we take to be instantiated with enormous frequency. Not for nothing did the existentialists make freedom the essence of our nature.[1] Doubtless the concept develops in us as part of our innate conceptual endowment, conditioning our whole conception of mind and action. Thus we take it for granted that human beings are confronted by a range of genuine alternatives, between which they must choose, and that their choices are free in the sense that they could have selected a distinct alternative from that which they actually selected. The agent is not compelled or constrained to act as he or she does, save in exceptional cases. We may be strongly inclined to do certain things, which makes it hard to do something else, yet we take ourselves to have the freedom to do what we are disinclined to do. We have a certain power to defy our natural propensities. So, at least, our commonsense view of action stoutly maintains: freedom is as real as consciousness or the self or meaning.

The trouble is that there seems to be a simple argument that shows that our prized freedom must be an illusion. The argument is exceedingly familiar, and runs as follows. Either determinism is true or it is not. If it is true, then all our chosen actions are uniquely necessitated by prior states of the world, just like every other event. But then it cannot be the case that we could have acted otherwise, since this would require a possibility determinism rules out. Once the initial conditions are set and the laws fixed, causality excludes genuine freedom. On the other hand, if indeterminism is true, then, though things could have happened otherwise, it is not the case that we could have chosen otherwise, since a merely random event is no kind of free choice.[2] That some events occur causelessly, or are not subject to law, or only to probabilistic law, is not sufficient for those events to be free choices. Thus one horn of the dilemma represents choices as predetermined happenings in a predictable causal sequence, while the other construes them as inexplicable lurches to which the universe is randomly prone. Neither alternative supplies what the notion of free will requires, and no other alternative suggests itself. Therefore freedom is not possible in any kind of possible world. The concept contains the seeds of its own destruction.

The problem centres upon the significance of the phrase 'could have done otherwise'. Determinism seems to imply that one could not do otherwise, while indeterminism gives the wrong interpretation to the phrase. Much has been written about this notion of possibility and its compatibility or otherwise with different global conceptions of the flow of events.[3] The problem has been to find a characterization of the freedom modality that shows how free choice is possible. What kind of power is signified by the idea that agents need not choose as they do? How can the natural world contain such a power? This is a question about a certain faculty that human beings possess, a certain natural attribute: what is the right theory of the structure and operation of this faculty? When an object possesses a power of a certain sort, expressible in modal terms, this will be grounded in certain objective properties of the object; the power depends upon the nature of what has it. Similarly, then, the freedom modality must have some inner nature and be related intelligibly to other properties of agents. It must, in particular, be somehow implemented by the machinery that implements our other psychological faculties – the machinery of the brain. And it must have a nature that is compatible with the facts about how human bodies work, deterministically or otherwise. The philosophical difficulty has been to produce such a characterization of the freedom modality.

Tautologically, to produce a characterization of something is to generate from one's actual conceptual scheme a set of propositions meeting certain epistemic conditions. So the problem can be said to be this: our conceptual scheme does not appear to yield a set of concepts that successfully captures the nature of the freedom modality. Such concepts as it does yield tend to make freedom look paradoxical and impossible – as with our concepts of the determined and the undetermined. By now we know what diagnosis TN will proffer of this state of affairs: in trying to produce a theory of the nature of freedom we run up against the limits and biases of our own cognitive system. Freedom is a phenomenon we can refer to but we cannot understand; the necessary theoretical concepts and principles fall outside the class of those that come naturally to us. Thus we fall into philosophical perplexity and cudgel our brains to find a way out. Straining at the bars of our cognitive cage, we concoct would-be solutions that never fully satisfy us, instead of accepting our cognitive predicament for what it is: so says TN. But before we explore the prospects for a TN position on free will further, we need to survey the relevant DIME options, noting their respective demerits.

II DIME and Free Will

Domesticating treatments of free will attempt to assimilate it to some independent model or paradigm of how events come about. The nexus of decision is taken to be just a special case of some other type of natural nexus; and the modality involved is not fundamentally different from other modalities represented in our scheme of concepts. Such reductive accounts take either a deterministic or an indeterministic form. The former type of theory insists that prior states of the world, consisting essentially in psychological states of the agent, are causally sufficient for a specific choice to be made, so that freedom comes out as a certain kind of causal sequence – that kind which features an appropriate set of mental antecedents. Freedom consists in causation by one's desires and beliefs.[4] The causal relation itself is nothing special; what differentiates free choice from its opposite is *what* does the causing. The latter type of theory rejects the attempt to reconcile freedom with determinism, claiming instead that only an acausal model can do justice to the freedom modality. When we say that an agent could have acted otherwise we must mean that the totality of prior conditions was consistent with any of a range of possible outcomes, so that a replication of that totality would not determine the choice made. We can preserve the modality only if we adopt a radically indeterministic model of choice. Thus it is sometimes held that quantum indeterminacy must be the root of freedom: random events at the subatomic level in the brain are the origin of free will.[5] These occur causelessly and are then amplified into grosser processes in brain tissue. Since the initiating event was not necessitated by the prior state of the world, we can say that the agent could have acted otherwise.

These are well-worn attempts to say what freedom consists in, and their difficulties are equally well-worn. The former type of theory does not give a sufficiently robust sense to the idea of the power to act otherwise, or gives it no sense at all, since it assimilates decision to any other kind of causal nexus. To say that one's actions are caused by one's beliefs and desires in the way that striking glass causes it to break does not allow room for the essential idea that the action is not necessitated by the beliefs and desires: the freedom modality drops out, and it cannot be reconstructed from the materials permitted by this type of account. The latter type of theory is best seen as a desperate response to the kind of problem just mentioned: we need groundfloor randomness in order to secure the independence of choice from what precedes it. Here the trouble is just that all we get by this manouevre is *mere* randomness, not the idea of an agent *doing* something. He is, as it were, the passive victim of the quantum leaps that erupt without cause in his brain matter. We lose the idea that the agent is in control of his actions; he is just the puppet of a randomness that occurs throughout the physical world. If we are to say that free choice is undetermined, it cannot be so in the way that quantum events are. So neither type of theory provides a satisfactory explanation of the power to act freely. The assimilations are deformations.[6]

Irreducibility theses are tailored to respect the *sui generis* status suggested by the failure of domesticating theories. Never explain; always distinguish. Our problem arises, the I theorist says, from trying to reduce what should be taken as primitive and self-intelligible: the freedom modality should not be forced into an alien conceptual mould; it is what it is and not another thing. Ordinary thought and speech attribute the power to act otherwise, treating free agents as a special ontological category; we should simply take this at face-value, resisting misplaced assimilations.[7] We can, if we like, introduce some semi-technical jargon in order to mark the distinctions we commonsensically make, calling free action a case of 'agent causation' rather than 'event causation'.[8] But we should not suppose that this provides any widening of the explanatory circle: we are simply recording the irreducible character of the power to act freely. The freedom modality is just one more specific kind of possibility to be added to the others we have to recognize – physical possibility, logical possibility, legal possibility, and so forth.

Here the central objection is that this position simply fails to meet the argument that seemed to put free will in jeopardy. Are human actions determined or are they not? If they are, then it is just not true that agents could do differently, no matter how irreducible the concept may be. But if they are not, then human action is just so much random meandering. We need a way of avoiding this argument, and the I position, as so far stated, is silent on the question. And this is before we get onto the usual questions about emergence and supervenience: how does the power to act freely relate to the biological nature of the agent, his brain apparatus, the law-governed sequences of bio-chemical events that occupy his interior? There are genuine explanatory questions here, and the I position dodges them.

Free will is perhaps the natural home of the non-naturalist. For surely, he will say, there is nothing in the experienced world that is quite so dramatically removed from the fixed routines of causality and predictability as an act of free choice. Each such action is itself a small miracle, contravening the dictates of the nomological order. The free agent has the power to hold back the tides of determinism, asserting his ascendancy over nature. In free choice we demonstrate the other-worldly aspect of our being. Choice is the natural expression of the soul, that supernatural entity that stands apart from the mechanics of matter. Thus religions typically see in choice our closest connection with God and his purposes: our faculty of choice has been divinely installed, with freedom built into it, so that we can live an ethically evaluable life. Not surprisingly, then, no naturalistic account can be given of the nature of freedom, and we sense the operations of the occult when we try to scrutinize it. Free choice does, indeed, resemble divine creation itself, in bringing something from nothing without prior constraint. We can only marvel at the miracle of freedom, never understand it.

This non-naturalism shares the defects of other attempts to invoke magical facts, but it also fails to answer the original argument. Are our supernatural souls determined or are they not? They may be immaterial and divinely tinged, but the same dilemma confronts them, as it does God himself. The anti-freedom argument needs to be undermined, and nothing in the present conception offers a way of doing that.

Elimination has seemed to many to be the only exit from the problem: the dilemma is unsolvable and freedom accordingly an illusion. The truth of general determinism by itself shows that there is no such thing as free action, so we need not even consider whether freedom is possible in an indeterministic universe. The concept of freedom may be central to the commonsense view of human action, and may be indispensable to moral evaluation, but it has been shown that the idea must be baseless, so we should eliminate it from our thought. No satisfactory sense can be made of the idea that agents could have acted otherwise.[9]

III TN and Free Will

TN says that there are such things as free choices but that we can form no adequate conception of their nature; the natural principles that underlie the power to do otherwise do not come within our theory-constructing capacities. We try to apply what concepts we have to the phenomenon, but they do not supply any satisfactory model of what is going on; our concepts of the undetermined, in particular, fail to do justice to the freedom modality. We are signally weak, constitutionally so, when it comes to forming concepts that would explain the nature of choice. Our philosophical perplexities result from this cognitive lack.

Is this position plausible? Can it help alleviate the conceptual pressures that threaten to destroy freedom? Well, there have been notable adherents of a TN position about the will. Hume writes, as part of his general realist agnosticism:

> The motion of our body follows upon the command of our will. Of this we are every moment conscious. But the means, by which this is effected; the energy, by which the will performs so extraordinary an operation; of this we are so far from being immediately conscious, that it must for ever escape our most diligent inquiry ... Were we empowered, by a secret wish, to remove mountains, or control the planets in their orbit; this extensive authority would not be more extraordinary, nor more beyond our comprehension ... We learn the influence of our will from experience alone. And experience only teaches us, how one event constantly follows another; without instructing us in the secret connection, which binds them together, and renders them inseparable.[10]

Kant, famously, holds that the will exists 'in a twofold sense', phenomenally and noumenally, saying:

> My soul, viewed from the latter standpoint, cannot indeed be known by means of speculative reason (and still less through empirical observation); and freedom as a property of a being to which I attribute effects in the sensible world, is therefore also not knowable in any such fashion . . . But though I cannot *know*, I can yet *think* freedom; that is to say, the representation of it is at least not self-contradictory, provided due account be taken of our critical distinction between the two modes of representation, the sensible and the intellectual, and of the resulting limitation of the pure concepts of understanding and of the principles which flow from them.[11]

Chomsky frequently cites the operations of will as belonging to his class of mysteries, which is why the theory of linguistic performance is so undeveloped and jejune, in contrast to theories of competence.[12] He says: 'Even the relevant concepts seem lacking; certainly, no intellectually satisfying principles have been proposed that have explanatory force, though the questions are very old. It is not excluded that human science-forming capacities simply do not extend to this domain, or any domain involving the exercise of will, so that for humans, these questions will always be shrouded in mystery.'[13] Elsewhere, referring to the creative aspect of language use, which he connects with freedom, he writes:

> One possible reason for the lack of success in solving it or even presenting sensible ideas about it is that it is not within the range of human intellectual capacities: It is either 'too difficult', given the nature of our capacities, or beyond their limits altogether. There is some reason to suspect that this may be so, though we do not know enough about human intelligence or the properties of the problem to be sure. We are able to devise theories to deal with strict determinacy and with randomness. But these concepts do not seem appropriate to Descartes's problem, and it may be that the relevant concepts are not accessible to us. A Martian scientist, with a mind different from ours, might regard this problem as trivial, and wonder why humans never seem to hit on the obvious way of solving it. This observer might also be amazed at the ability of every human child to acquire language, something that seems to him incomprehensible, requiring divine intervention,

because the elements of the language faculty lie beyond his conceptual range.[14]

This perfectly expresses the TN standpoint and might be taken as a text for the general position we are exploring. The Chomskian hypothesis is that our incomprehension regarding the will, though probably terminal, is a product of our peculiar cognitive make-up, the conceptual resources contingently at our command; it does not indicate any objective profundity or divine design. The problem stems from the particular properties of human cognition. Some science details the principles governing the will, including its relation to our biological nature, but that science is not available to our theoretical faculties. Thus we label the problem 'philosophical'.

As hitherto, one of the chief merits of TN is avoidance of the DIME trap; it provides an escape from the usual unpalatable alternatives. But before we contemplate this method of escape we need to assure ourselves that free will is not already ruled out by any of the standard arguments; we need, in particular, to consider the old question of the compatibility of freedom with determinism. For TN has no power to save what can be *demonstrated* to be impossible or nonexistent. The question, then, is whether the kind of necessitation consequent upon the truth of determinism is consistent with the kind of possibility required by the freedom modality: could the agent have done otherwise given that he had to do what he did? Can the existence of genuine alternatives be reconciled with the fixity entailed by determinism?

It can certainly seem like we have a straight contradiction here, since what is necessarily not so cannot be possibly so; but modal truths are notoriously tricky and equivocal, so let us see whether we can remove the appearance of contradiction. To say that an action is free is, I suggest, to make a relational claim: freedom is freedom *from* certain things. We can express this idea in terms of supervenience: the action is not supervenient on the body of facts in question, in the sense that the action could be different without that body of facts being different. Now the crucial question is whether the notion of freedom requires nonsupervenience on *all* facts or only on *some*. For, if it requires global nonsupervenience, then indeed it is hard to reconcile freedom with determinism; but, if it requires only a more local nonsupervenience, then it might be consistent with some varieties of determinism and not others. Then two sets of facts on which choices might or might not supervene are physical facts and mental facts. If you fix all the physical facts, do you thereby fix the choices? And if you fix all the mental facts, not counting the choices themselves, do you fix the choices? In other words, must physical duplicates perform the same actions, and must mental duplicates do so? My suggestion is this: the ordinary notion of freedom requires mental nonsupervenience, and this is not ruled out by any fundamental principle, but it does not require physical nonsupervenience, which is fortunate because that does seem hard to deny. It does not, on this view, follow from the necessity for physical duplicates to act in the same way that they are not free, but that would follow if it were true of mental duplicates: however, it is not true. Let me now defend this suggestion.

I think that when we say a person acted freely we mean that, given his set of desires and other attitudes, his choice was not yet fixed. His desires inclined him, perhaps strongly, to make a certain choice, but in fact it was really possible for him to resist those desires and do something else. He could have done otherwise, that is, relative to his total set of attitudes: they do not necessitate a particular action. The ability to overrule desire is what the ordinary notion is mainly about. This does not imply anything about the nonsupervenience of choice upon the agent's total physical condition; it is strictly a claim about psychology, about the looseness between desire and choice. So it is not incompatible with physical determinism. Two agents who are alike mentally may perform different actions and there be a corresponding physical difference between them, one that has no manifestation at the level of desire. But it is far from clear that ordinary ascriptions of freedom are intended to be incompatible with physical supervenience: no such recondite thought seems implied. Thus it is consistent with freedom, as we ordinarily conceive of it, that physical duplicates must act identically. The folk psychology of 'free' is neutral on the question of physical determinism.

This claim is bound to seem unsatisfactory if we insist, misguidedly, on construing physical supervenience as an explanatory relation. Focusing on the underlying physiology, and supposing this to be what the exercise of will really consists in, we will find it hard to preserve the notion of an agent's free choice. But it is a mistake to think that the *nature* of choice is revealed in what it supervenes upon. There is no reason to suppose that the principles of choice are constructable from its physical supervenience base.[15] What TN says is that we are fundamentally ignorant about what freedom consists in, so that we are prone to fill the gap in our understanding with misleading models and metaphors, which undermine what they are designed to explain. The neural correlates of choice, as we conceive them, do not supply us with a theory of what choice is; so freedom cannot be undermined by observing that these correlates are not themselves free – that would be a confusion of levels. We simply do not understand how the necessities of matter are related to the possibilities of will, so all inferences from the former to the latter are suspect. In particular, we cannot infer that the will is not free from the fact that all actions are physically necessitated: the ordinary notion does not deny this, and physical processes provide no explanatory model of the kind of thing the will is. The danger in this subject is to assume that we know more about what constitutes the will than we really do, subsuming it under concepts that misrepresent its nature.[16]

I said just now that the essence of freedom is the 'looseness' that obtains between choice and desire. This is the point at which we reach for the idea of the undetermined, but quickly find that this leads only to an abyss of incomprehension. The CALM conjecture has something to say about this: our trouble (or part of it) is that the relation in question – that between desire and decision – is not representable in CALM terms. There are two reasons why not. First, our notion of the lawlike fails at this point, as does our notion of causality: the production of decision is quite unlike the production of motion and the like – even to speak of 'production' here rings false. Second, the combinatorial paradigm runs aground in this case: decisions are not compounds of antecedent desires and other attitudes, nor of brain states. Undoubtedly there are links here, but they cannot be made unmysterious by means of CALM relations. Hence the feeling that decision involves radical novelty, a transition to something of another order altogether. This signals our inability to bring CALM to the phenomena.

Yet it must not be forgotten that free will is a natural phenomenon, rooted in biology. Children acquire it spontaneously,
presumably by way of their innate endowment. Human beings
have the capacity to digest food by virtue of mechanisms inside
them; similarly they have the capacity to act freely in virtue of
their biological nature. That we understand the former but are
completely clueless about the latter is no reason to suppose any
difference at the level of ontology; the difference is an epistemological one.[17] As Chomsky says, Martians might find the free will
problem trivial in comparison to the digestion problem, given
their cognitive slant. The capacity to act freely develops in us by
a series of natural steps, implemented somehow by structures in
our nervous system, rather as our capacity to speak does – indeed,
the two capacities are interwoven. What does not develop naturally
in us is the capacity to *understand* this capacity. One might even
be forgiven for suspecting that we develop capacities for *not*
understanding free will, these being geared to phenomena of quite
other types. Hence we style the problem 'philosophical'.

Finally, some remarks about how TN bears upon our practice
of praise and blame. Kant writes: 'Morality does not, indeed,
require that freedom should be understood, but only that it should
not contradict itself, and so should at least allow of being thought,
and that as thus thought it should place no obstacle in the way
of a free act (viewed in another relation) likewise conforming to
the mechanism of nature.'[18] Paraphrasing, Kant's point is that
rational praise and blame require only that we know free will to
exist, not that we grasp its nature. This is clearly correct, but the
inadequacy of our understanding of freedom, and our propensity
to distort it when we attempt to frame a theory of its nature, are
bound to affect our sense of the justification of praise and blame.
Ethical evaluation depends upon something murky and elusive to
us, lying athwart our inbuilt categories of understanding. It is
thus natural (though mistaken) to entertain sceptical suspicions
about free will, and hence the moral and political practices that
presuppose its reality. Such suspicions might be allayed by the
assumption of a divine authority who vouches for the existence
of what we cannot comprehend, but in the absence of this as-
surance doubts are only to be expected. Perhaps, however, a clear
acknowlegement of TN about freedom can help keep these doubts

at bay: for we can explain their prevalence without misconstruing or exaggerating their import. If our theoretical failings in respect of the phenomenon are seen for what they are, namely results of our specific cognitive deficiencies, not symptoms of objective incoherence, then we can continue to accept, at a reflective level, what we spontaneously believe – that human agents are free and responsible. We need not succumb to eliminativist doubts. Accepting TN can thus help us preserve ethical evaluation, with all that that implies, while agreeing that it depends upon something that necessarily escapes our theoretical comprehension.

NOTES

1   See Jean-Paul Sartre, *Being and Nothingness*. Freedom, according to Sartre, is intimately bound up with consciousness and intentionality.
2   I am not endorsing this move from the undetermined to the random, but it is natural to feel its pull when we try – contrary to the spirit of TN – to give positive theoretical content to the category of the undetermined.
3   See the collection *Essays on Freedom of Action*, ed. Ted Honderich.
4   See Davidson, 'Freedom to Act'.
5   See John Eccles and Karl Popper, *The Self and its Brain*.
6   See Galen Strawson, *Freedom and Belief*; Thomas Nagel, *The View From Nowhere*, chapter 7.
7   See P. F. Strawson, 'Freedom and Resentment'.
8   Davidson discusses this in 'Agency'.
9   I suspect that a large proportion of the thinking population currently accepts this: here eliminativism has made its way into the mainstream – along with atheism.
10   Hume, *Enquiry Concerning Human Understanding*, pp. 64–5.
11   Kant, *Critique of Pure Reason*, p. 28.
12   In this respect, as in others, Chomsky follows the example of Descartes: see *Language and Problems of Knowledge*, p. 140.
13   Chomsky, *Reflections on Language*, p. 25.
14   Chomsky, *Language and Problems of Knowledge*, pp. 151–2.
15   This is really just to insist upon the explanatory autonomy of the special sciences – despite a general supervenience on the physical.
16   This is particularly true with respect to the causal concepts we apply to the mind. The concept of cause, properly understood, is highly schematic, and there is thus a persistent tendency to thicken

it in the direction of paradigms that may not fit the case we are considering. Certainly, it is a mistake to inflate the common application of causal concepts to mental and physical phenomena into a *theory* of the workings of the mind. That beliefs and desires cause actions tells us next to nothing about the principles involved; it makes no significant dent in our theoretical ignorance.

17   I am not, of course, denying that choices are mental and digestion is physical; I mean only that their relative mysteriousness is a purely epistemological matter. The same point could be made about our general sense that the mind is somehow intrinsically *odder* than the body.

18   Kant, *Critique of Pure Reason*, p. 29.

6

The A Priori

I The Problem: Ungrounded Knowledge

Part of our commonsense view of ourselves is that we have knowledge of diverse kinds. We have a range of epistemic capacities, innately based, which interact with our learning history to produce well-founded beliefs about a variety of subject-matters. A central philosophical concern has been to understand how we come to have this extensive and heterogeneous system of knowledge. How is it possible for human beings, constituted and located as they are, to have the kind of knowledge they appear to possess? What explains this? The question is philosophical because there seem to be obstacles of principle in the way of human knowledge: it is problematic that we should have the knowledge we have; by rights we ought not to be so epistemically accomplished. From a theoretical perspective, it is a startling fact about us that we know as much as we do; much more startling than, say, our running and lifting abilities, where the enabling processes and mechanisms are transparent enough not to invite philosophical perplexity.[1]

The philosophical problem about knowledge has two main forms, marked deep into the history of the subject. First there is the general problem of scepticism, powered by the suspicion that our reasons for the knowledge claims we make fall woefully short of the content of those claims: this is essentially a problem of underdetermination, of the 'input' failing to warrant the 'output'. Secondly, there is a more restricted problem about certain kinds of knowledge, which is anterior to sceptical problems: this is the problem of explaining how we come to have the kind of knowledge traditionally labelled 'a priori'. The next chapter will deal with the former problem; this chapter addresses the latter – the problem of how a priori knowledge is possible.

Why is this a particular problem? The answer can be extracted from the traditional definition of the a priori: in contrast to a posteriori knowledge, a priori knowledge is the kind that is not based on experience. Our knowledge of logic, mathematics, meaning and so on is derived from some other source, not from the deliverances of our senses and certain principles of inference therefrom. We do not direct our sensory organs at the fact to be known, thus registering its presence; nor do we infer the fact from what is so detectable. A priori knowledge thus differs essentially and qualitatively from empirical knowledge. Putting the matter in current jargon, a priori knowledge is not derived by way of a causally mediated input–output transaction: it does not originate by taking some externally derived impingement of energy and mapping this onto an appropriate cognitive output. The a priori faculty skips the operations of the perceptual systems, regarding them as strictly irrelevant to its proper concerns, and simply proceeds in its own self-sufficient way, generating an impressive end-result. It does its job in a causally autonomous way. We might even define a priori knowledge as the kind that we have independently of standing in naturalistic causal relations to the subject-matter of our knowledge.[2] Indeed, the ontology typical of propositions known a priori – namely, abstract entities – is of a kind to shun causal relations altogether. Numbers, say, do not relate to our a priori faculties as material objects relate to our empirical faculties. In short, broadly causal epistemology, predicated upon naturalistic interactions between fact and faculty, breaks down in the case of a priori knowledge. It is not so much that the stimulus is impoverished or inadequate to what it prompts; rather, the whole notion of a stimulus to knowledge is out of place – just not part of how the a priori faculty works. Here knowledge seems to be generated *ex nihilo*, in a feat of pure creativity, as if the mind could leap to the fact known without any mediation or assistance. A priori knowledge presents itself as splendidly aloof from the world of causal interactions, fortuitous impingements, extraneous linkages. It is the knowledge of the solipsist, available to any mind of sufficient inner power, irrespective of luck or location. Its essence is to be independent of the empirical flux.

This sounds like a good way for knowledge to be, which is why strands in the tradition treat the a priori as privileged and paradigmatic, but it poses massive problems of explanatory inclusion. For, in so distancing a priori knowledge from the empirical variety, this conception leaves us without any explanatory model for how such knowledge *does* arise; all we are told is that it is *not* derived in the causal–experiential style. The question then is what other kind of explanation it might have: how do states of the faculty connect up (if that is the word) with the subject-matter of what is known? What are the mechanisms, the processes, the enabling conditions?[3]

That way of characterizing the a priori, and the theoretical challenge it presents, is reminiscent of the problem of free will. Free will also has a kind of stimulus-independence or causal autonomy, as if it is not subject to the usual rules of natural production: choices are not simply the effect or output of antecedent circumstances; they enter the world in a self-propelled manner. Not surprisingly, then, the tell-tale notion of creativity is regularly invoked (however blankly) in order to gesture at the oddity of both a priori knowledge and acts of will. Something, in both cases, appears to be coming from nothing. Both challenge our usual causal–nomological–mechanistic picture of the world: some things seem to happen without the help of law-governed sequences of states, each proceeding from earlier ones by the power of good old-fashioned causation. Free will and the a priori introduce causal clefts at points where no other notion suggests itself: between choice and desire, knowledge and fact. The world appears to be working in ways that defy our usual theoretical tools, and we are left characterizing both phenomena negatively – as *not* subject to causation as we normally understand it. It may well be, then, that free will and a priori knowledge are both tapping the same vein of intellectual ineptitude. They both consist in the holding of relations that baffle our understanding.

Let me restate the problem in slightly different terms, bringing out the structural divergence between empirical and a priori knowledge, and hence the explanatory puzzle presented by the latter. In the case of knowledge based on experience we have a three-stage set-up: there is the fact, the state of knowledge, and an experience that mediates the two. The fact produces the experience (or is connected suitably to a fact that does) which in turn produces the knowledge state; so the experience is what points the mind in the right cognitive direction, connecting it to the world known about. It is highly natural, indeed unavoidable, to conceive this double relation in causal terms, thus assimilating the generation of empirical knowledge to other mediated causal sequences in the world. But in the case of non-empirical knowledge we cannot conceive of its production in anything like these terms: a mathematical fact, say, does not first cause an experience in us by means of sensory transducers, which in turn produces mathematical knowledge. Nothing of that mediating and knowledge-securing kind occurs. So we are at a loss to model the acquisition of such knowledge on our general conception of causal sequence; here the world is not laid out in a series of intelligibly connected causal processes. Accordingly, we cannot say what kind of natural structure or process is exemplified when the a priori faculty operates. In the case of this type of knowledge, it is tempting to say, *we just have it* – immediately, acausally, unanalysably. But, of course, this is to say nothing, save that it cannot be modelled upon processes of which we possess an intelligible conception. It is, in short, a characteristically philosophical puzzle – a puzzle about how the world *could* contain such a thing. We have no clear idea about how the mind might be operating when it succeeds in locking onto the kinds of fact proper to a priori knowledge – not even the rudiments.

It would be wrong to think that the problem attaches only to some small and peripheral area of knowledge, sealed off from the bulk of what we know. Apart from the fact that the (traditional) list of types of a priori knowledge is rather long and substantial – all of mathematics to begin with – it must also be recognized that traces of the a priori enter into our every thought. All knowledge, arguably, draws upon the contents of the a priori faculty. This is because all knowledge involves some appreciation of logical relations, implicitly at least. To know a given proposition one must have some awareness of what other propositions it entails and excludes; and this requires a grasp of logical principles, themselves known a priori. Thus even the most brutally empirical knowledge is embedded in a background of a priori knowledge.[4] So the mystery of the a priori attaches to knowledge quite generally.

II DIME and the A Priori

A large part of the modern period of philosophy has been devoted to struggling with the problem of the a priori, and a great many positions have been proposed. As heretofore a brief survey must suffice, designed to highlight the broad topography of the issue in readiness for TN.

Domesticating theories tend to come in two forms or to combine two strands. A priori knowledge is held to be either (i) more trivial in content than we are initially tempted to suppose, and/ or (ii) closer to ordinary empirical knowledge than it seems. Thus it is said that nothing 'factual' is known a priori, and that what is thus known is really just a special case of a posteriori knowledge (these two ideas pull in opposite directions, of course). Some have accordingly held that a priori truths really concern mental entities of some sort ('concepts'), so that our knowledge of them resolves into a special case of self-knowledge – it is merely knowledge of what lies within.[5] Others, similarly motivated, have assimilated all a priori knowledge to knowledge of language, calling a priori truths 'analytic', and locating their source in what words mean.[6] Perhaps sensing that this is not quite tame enough, ontologically and epistemologically, more radical thinkers have insisted that a priori knowledge reduces to knowledge of human conventions – decisions or declarations about what to cleave to or permit or concur in.[7] Just to be on the safe side, some of these thinkers have taken the syntactic turn, claiming that a priori truth is covertly 'formal' – a matter of empty symbols and their purely formal relations.[8] (Compare the adoption of 'syntactic' theories of mind in the face of the perplexities of intentionality).[9] At the far end of this domesticating spectrum we have the idea that a priori knowledge is as trivial as purely orthographic knowledge and as empirically founded as it is. Arithmetic, say, is all just a matter of marks on paper: one perceives the marks and develops skills in manipulating them, and that is what mathematical knowledge ultimately comes down to. We do not need to countenance inscrutable apprehensions of a non-spatial non-causal world of abstract entities.

Finding such reductive theories implausible, one turns next to an irreducibility claim. The philosophical problem stems from taking empirical knowledge as the standard for all genuine knowledge; predictably, then, the a priori comes out looking difficult or impossible. The remedy is to accept the a priori on its own terms, not to seek some kind of explanation or model of how it works. After all, we have a name for the faculty in question, *viz.*, 'reason', and we can distinguish this from the sensory faculties – the concepts are in good order as they stand. We know how to sort items of knowledge into one category or the other; our schools teach children arithmetic perfectly adequately; mathematicians prove their theorems and become celebrated. These facts are not going to be compromised by a philosophical bewilderment that issues from misplaced explanatory ambitions. The knowledge we derive by the mere exercise of reason is distinguished by just that; there is no point in fretting about the undeniable dissimilarities between this kind of knowledge and knowledge of other types. Dogmatic reductionism is the cause of the trouble, not a priori knowledge itself.[10]

The thinness and blinkeredness of the I position, its avoidance of the question what reason *is*, might now pitch us in the direction of an honest supernaturalism. Let us candidly admit that a priori knowledge confutes dogmatic naturalism: it does indeed call for the attribution of non-natural mental faculties, capable of reaching out beyond space and the causal order. As divine revelation acquaints us with God, so the abstract world is revealed to us by miraculous methods. Plato advocated just such a view, and there is more than a whiff of it in Gödel's contention that we possess a special faculty of mathematical intuition that puts us in touch, inexplicably, with abstract reality.[11] Our minds are more than causally driven engines, subject to the usual laws of nature; we are all seers of a sort, capable of mystic visions. In gaining a priori knowledge we manifest our non-natural essence, our freedom from the grubby sublunary world.

Recoiling from the extravagance – or worse, vapidity – of M

doctrines, eliminativism offers its own drastic brand of resolution. There is no a priori knowledge! Eliminativists tend to come in two kinds, one more radical than the other. The less radical kind allows that there is (say) mathematical knowledge but denies that it is a priori in any substantive sense. It is continuous with empirical knowledge, merely more general or highly confirmed, less likely to be given up when experience proves recalcitrant.[12] The subject-matter may be abstract, but we know it in virtue of its theoretical links to other empirical knowledge – the only kind of knowledge there can be. All knowledge is based on experience, but some is inferentially close to experience and some is distant. The more radical eliminativist denies that we are dealing with *knowledge* at all, with true propositions that describe a particular sector of reality.[13] Mathematical sentences are not truth-bearers; numbers do not exist; there is no genuine knowledge of mathematics. The sentences in question have a different kind of status, as does our cognitive relation to them: perhaps they prescribe rules of a certain sort, or are pieces in a game, or function fictionally. In any case, there are no a priori *facts* with respect to which our epistemic relation could be deemed problematic. If mathematics *were* known, then it would have to be known a priori, and might then call for a magical metaphysics: but since it is not known to begin with, we do not have to fret over the consequences of accepting such knowledge.

It is worth noting separately that ethical knowledge, often classified as a priori, has provoked an analogous set of responses.[14] We would like to know how ethical knowledge is possible, given its apparent remoteness from the sensory and scientific. Some say, in a domesticating spirit, that ethical knowledge is knowledge of certain natural facts, say about desires or the distribution of happiness. Others declare that knowledge of ethical truth must be seen as irreducibly normative, that it is a mistake to assimilate it to other forms of knowledge. Yet others believe that the ethical is a direct reflection of the divine: since ethical truth is a matter of God's edicts, our knowledge of it must be divinely mediated. Then there are those who deny that truth can be properly attributed to ethical sentences, holding instead that ethical utterances are exclamatory or hortatory or merely windy; these non-cognitivists hold precisely that there is no such thing as ethical knowledge. Thus putative ethical knowledge fits the general DIME shape characteristic of the a priori. Knowledge of the normative poses much the same kinds of problem as knowledge of the abstract: for how do facts about what *ought* to be so impinge on our faculties in such a way as to produce the corresponding states of knowledge? Only what *is* so can do any causal impinging. Retinae do not resonate to the right.

III   TN and A Priori Knowledge

The usual pattern is repeating itself: the world appears to contain a certain kind of phenomenon – a priori knowledge in this case – radically different in nature from other phenomena, and the philosophical task is to give some account of what this phenomenon consists in, explaining how it is possible for the world to contain it. The DIME shape lays out the range of responses to the problem that have seemed attractive or inevitable; and TN steps in to challenge the exhaustiveness and relative plausibility of these standard responses. In the case of the a priori, then, we should expect TN to motivate itself in the customary way – by pressing its claim to put the epistemology of the situation in the right light. What is plain is that we have great difficulty forming any transparent explanatory picture of the operations of the a priori faculty: specifically, we cannot find a suitable naturalistic characterization of the relation between the facts known and our knowledge of them. Crudely, we cannot represent the knower as spatially and causally related to the entities he knows about, cognitively keyed onto them via an intermediate experiential state. The metaphor of mental vision, so appealing in depicting the a priori, lacks the naturalistic structure of vision proper, with its causal interactions and spatial relatedness. Talk of 'vision' here is quite unexplanatory, a mere gesture in the general direction of what we find intelligible. Thus the notion of a priori knowledge covers an area of epistemological blankness, a place where our theoretical powers cannot enter. The notion thereby becomes philosophically problematic.

TN accepts this initial description of the problem at face-value, and offers a distinctive diagnosis of our difficulty. Instead of warping the phenomenon to fit our contingent conceptual resources in a (laudable) effort to save its reality, or declaring it ontologically brute, or proclaiming its mystical underpinnings, or just denying its very existence, TN proposes fully to accept its reality while acknowledging that we cannot in principle give any account of it. A priori knowledge has an objective nature, a set of naturalistic enabling conditions, but it just so happens that our cognitive slant is ill-suited to discovering and articulating what this consists in. We thus tend to paper over the explanatory gap with metaphors, analogies, hyperbole, in a vain attempt to get the structure of the phenomenon into focus. Our specific modes of understanding do not penetrate into the nature of our own ability to acquire knowledge of this type. We are like three-dimensional beings equipped with only two-dimensional concepts. Deep-going theoretical bafflement is the natural response to this predicament – philosophy, in other words.

In the case of empirical knowledge, we at least understand the *kind* of thing we are dealing with: we can see how to map such knowledge onto its objects by way of certain naturalistic relations. Thus we can bring a measure of CALM to the phenomenon: objects in space send out signals that intersect the paths of cognitively receptive beings, irritating their senses, and ultimately rearranging their internal cognitive states. This model works well for basic perceptual knowledge, but it also extends quite smoothly to much more inferential knowledge – of the past, the future, the microscopic, the distant. Knower and known co-exist within a matrix of spatial and causal relations, exhibiting systematic dependencies between them – all of this falling within our general mode of understanding of how the world works. We can thus keep relatively CALM in the presence of empirical knowledge.[15] But when it comes to a priori knowledge the CALM format lets us down rather dramatically: we cannot so much as formulate the type of relation that permits our minds to make contact with the facts we apparently know. Assuming these facts to be abstract, we cannot even locate us and them in the same sector of reality! There is no mediating structure (that we can discern) that maps the abstract world onto our cognitive states; the relation appears inexplicable, a blank confrontation of opposites. Theoretically, it resembles the problematic relation between consciousness and the brain: here too there has to be *some* intelligible explanatory link, but its nature remains elusive to us. TN says that the link is objectively there all right but that it does not fit the mould of our thought. Beings of a different theoretical constitution might find the link quite transparent to them, thus relegating the investigation of a priori knowledge to normal science as they understand it; for them, the profoundest philosophy might attach, rather, to the kind of knowledge we find relatively intelligible – knowledge of the perceptible properties of nearby material objects.[16] Intelligibility, after all, is always a function of the particular conceptual resources with which one is naturally endowed.

I think it is natural to feel, in this case almost more than in any of the others I have discussed, that the prospects for TN's truth are uniquely dim, on account of the seemingly paradoxical character of a priori knowledge as we have characterized it. For TN cannot make what is intrinsically incoherent into a properly behaved item in our world inventory. And a priori knowledge has the look of actual incoherence, of asking the impossible, not merely that of raising profound questions about its own possibility. This is most apparent when we focus on the nature of abstract entities, the putative objects of such knowledge. Let me then first try to formulate the felt impossibility, before making a suggestion about what it would take to resolve it. Abstract entities, such as numbers, evidently have no spatial location, are not subject to intrinsic change, and lack causal powers; but knowers, such as ourselves, have all three of these characteristics, notably as regards our minds. Yet somehow, if we are to have knowledge of abstract entities, we must come into cognitive contact with them. And the trouble is that no conceivable mode of contact seems feasible between entities of such radically different kinds – you might as well say that we can kick or squash abstract entities! The case is thus rather worse than that of consciousness and the brain, since at least in that case the two entities share the three sorts of characteristic mentioned. It seems paradoxical that we, constituted as we are, could make epistemic contact with numbers (say) constituted as they are. If TN is to be in the running, therefore, it needs to show that the apparent paradox is unreal; that this is a case of an impenetrable possibility rather than that of a demonstrable impossibility.

Three points may be made about this, in ascending order of speculativeness. First, there is no logical inconsistency in the characterization of a priori knowledge, so nothing of the order of a formal paradox; it is more that there seems to be no non-magical way to make the crossing from the concrete to the abstract that the a priori requires. If we think of the a priori faculty as a kind of perceptual system, then it implies the admittedly puzzling – but not actually contradictory – idea that there can be perception of entities in the absence of both causal connection and spatial co-relatedness. This certainly departs from the ordinary notion of empirical perception, but it would be tendentious in the present context to insist that the resulting notion is internally incoherent; and besides we are not obliged to use the word 'perception' literally when describing the operations of the a priori faculty.

Second, we cannot take it for granted that our grip on the nature of the abstract realm is objectively comprehensive or deep. Perhaps our concepts of the abstract are glancing and superficial, revealing only certain aspects of their referents – rather as I have suggested that our concepts of consciousness are.[17] We know a good many truths about numbers, say, but our general concept of their ontological category might be inadequate to penetrating their real objective nature. After all, we are nothing if not spatial beings, our modes of conception suffused with spatial content, while the abstract is essentially non-spatial: maybe then we are fundamentally limited or skewed in our thought about the abstract by dint of our spatially oriented forms of understanding. Other beings, less spatially immersed, might have conceptions of numbers and the like that differ significantly from ours, allowing them to form theories of their place in the world that are closed to us. These beings might then be much better placed to understand how knowledge of the abstract is possible. TN about the abstract itself may thus play a part in blocking human understanding of human knowledge of that domain.[18] Certainly our attempts to define the category of the abstract are apt to be distressingly negative in form, as when we declare it *not* spatial or causal; we have little positive or illuminating to say about the notion.

Third, part of the problem stems from picturing abstract entities and structures as *outside* the mind, so that our mental faculties need to span some kind of abyss in order to afford knowledge of them. But this assumption should not be accepted uncritically; there may be other theoretical possibilities which, though not pellucid in themselves, offer a less paradoxical vision of how the a priori faculty might be working, at least in broad outline. One suggestion, by no means unprecedented, is that a priori knowledge is really inwardly directed: it is knowledge of properties of one's own mind. I do not mean to be broaching the old theory that it is knowledge of one's intentions or dispositions to linguistic behaviour; I mean to be introducing a much more surprising idea, at least according to current conceptions. The idea is that in ways we do not comprehend the abstract world enters into the very nature of our minds: reason is somehow *constituted* by the abstract entities to which it also enjoys epistemic access. The merit of this suggestion, odd though it may sound, is that it shakes the hold of the idea that the mind must magically reach outside itself into another sector of reality altogether in order to acquire a priori knowledge, where this reaching out has no intelligible mediation. We might do better, in assuring the possibility of a priori knowledge, to locate its objects *inside* the mind, so that the requisite faculties have no unbreachable barrier to cross. Then a priori knowledge is the abstract nature of mind imprinting itself on our epistemic faculties. It is not that this suggestion is itself theoretically transparent; in the context of a defence of TN that is hardly to be expected. The point is rather that if anything like this were true, whether or not we can properly appreciate its truth, it would help in easing acceptance of the possibility of knowledge of the abstract. And I venture to suggest that, in this area, we should err on the side of boldness, trying out any possibility that stands a chance of saving the phenomena.

It is natural to seek a unified picture of reality, in which the mental, the physical and the abstract are all intelligibly related. We want to be able to represent these large ontological junctures as meshing smoothly with each other – with no bumps or anomalies or antinomies. The problem of the a priori is one aspect of this larger problem. According to TN, we are not going to arrive at this unified theory, because of our inbuilt conceptual limitations or biases. However, it by no means follows that we have to revise any of our ordinary beliefs about the kinds of thing the world contains: we are not required to reject what we cannot explain. What TN offers is ontological breathing space, the freedom to accept what is terminally baffling. We can thus continue to believe in a priori knowledge without being able to provide any account of what makes it possible. This is just to acknowledge that reason is not capable of producing a full theory of itself.

NOTES

1 There are, of course, unsolved scientific questions about these motor abilities, but it is not commonly supposed that these are such as to put the very existence of the abilities in doubt: no one is a sceptic about running and lifting. But our epistemic abilities have been thought far less secure, to the point where their very possibility is cast into doubt. It is worth pondering the reasons for this kind of assumed asymmetry.

2 I defined the a priori in this way in 'A Priori and A Posteriori Knowledge'.

3 Compare Paul Benacerraf, 'Mathematical Truth'.

4 Applied mathematics is another case in point, both in science and everyday life. Actually, I think that ordinary human experience is far more shot through with mathematical content than empiricist philosophers have wished to acknowledge: even simple visual perception has numerical notions built into it, as we apply concepts of number to the pluralities we perceive – not to mention geometry and our spatial awareness. Our perceptual and mathematical faculties are more intertwined than enthusiasts of the a posteriori have allowed.

5 Thus Hume's 'relations of ideas', psychologically conceived, are taken to be the direct objects of a priori knowledge: see *A Treatise of Human Nature*, Part III, section 1.

6 This is the standard linguistic conception of a priori knowledge common among positivists and others.

7 See A. J. Ayer, *Language, Truth and Logic*.

8 Thus the mathematical formalists such as David Hilbert.

9 Stephen Stich, *From Folk Psychology to Cognitive Science*.

10 This is the type of view one associates with the 'ordinary language' philosophers, though I know of no actual source expressly stating the view.

11 Kurt Gödel, 'What is Cantor's Continuum Problem?'

12 W. V. Quine, 'Two Dogmas of Empiricism'.

13   Hartry Field defends this position in *Science Without Numbers*.

14   Russell so classifies ethical knowledge in *The Problems of Philosophy*, pp. 75–6.

15   I say 'relatively' because empirical knowledge also poses its own problems of principle, as we shall see in the next chapter.

16   Incompetence in the employment of spatial concepts would be enough to produce this result, as with Strawson's conceptually truncated sound beings: see *Individuals*, chapter 2. Contemplating these beings is a good way not to take our spatial concepts for granted – and hence our particular perspective on the world.

17   See chapter 2 and 'The Hidden Structure of Consciousness'.

18   Even the most ardent realists about abstract entities do not seem willing to entertain the kind of epistemic closure or partialness I am envisaging; some sort of transparent and immediate access is the usual assumption. But it is not clear what, for a realist about the abstract, could motivate this kind of epistemological optimism. Why shouldn't objectively existing abstract entities be only incompletely grasped by us – even in respect of their fundamental nature? What reason is there to deny that what is intrinsically mind-independent might have a deep nature that is not accessible to our thought? Why can't the abstract have a noumenal side?

7

Knowledge

I The Problem: How Do We Know Anything?

In the previous chapter I said that a priori knowledge is peculiarly problematic relative to empirical knowledge; but this is not
to say that the latter type of knowledge is quite unproblematic.
And, of course, empirical knowledge itself has been thought to
raise deep problems with respect to its very possibility. In this
chapter I shall investigate whether TN can be profitably applied
to the philosophical problem of knowledge more generally; in
particular, I shall be concerned with the problem of scepticism.
Can knowledge be saved from scepticism by invoking a TN thesis
about its enabling conditions?

The concept of knowledge is perhaps the most philosophically
fragile concept in our repertoire of basic concepts. Common sense
takes knowledge to be both possible and widespread, simply part
of life. People (and some animals) are assumed to know a great
many things across a broad range of subject-matters. The purpose of education, including much speech, is the inculcation of
knowledge. We regard the acquisition of knowledge as especially
valuable, some people devoting their lives to its increase and
dissemination. But it takes very little reflection, or prompting, to
cast all this into serious doubt: we quickly come to feel that the
concept lacks the kind of broad and ready application we earlier
took for granted. Sceptical thoughts occur readily and with considerable force, soon leading us to declare that, after all, we
know little or nothing. The concept strikes us as containing the

seeds of its own destruction, by requiring the satisfaction of conditions that are palpably unsatisfied. Ontogenetically, the concept of knowledge comes into play during the first three or four years, but it is apt to lose its moorings during adolescence, when reflection intrudes. Then it is commonly asserted, with the air of the platitudinous, that of course nobody every really *knows* anything. How could they, given the content of the concept and the facts of epistemic life? Philosophical scepticism thus seems endemic to the use of epistemic concepts: to reflect on the concept of knowledge is immediately to question its application. Not surprisingly, then, scepticism arose early in the history of philosophical thought and has continued to exercise a powerful hold on it. I hazard the anthropological conjecture that every culture has its sceptics, silent though they may be. There is something primitive and inevitable about sceptical doubt. It runs deep in human thought. The question is whether it can be overcome, and by what means.[1]

The sceptical train of thought can take both a first-person and a third-person form. The first-person form is probably more basic and immediate, going to the nerve of what makes scepticism as powerful as it is. Naively stated, it is the feeling that I cannot, by means of my basic modes of awareness, get beyond my own inner experience, my own subjective world. I am trapped, epistemically, within my present state of consciousness. The boundaries of what I truly know are coterminus with the limits of my phenomenal experience; anything else I see fit to assent to is at best so much shaky inference from this secure foundation. Acquaintance stops with self-awareness, so that what is immediately present to me is never anything logically independent of the contents of my consciousness. It is in the very nature of consciousness that my epistemic powers should be thus restricted. Accordingly, knowledge claims should be confined to those that are solipsistically certifiable – those that could hold even if I were the only existent thing. My epistemic faculties cannot take me outside how things subjectively seem to me.

The third-person route to scepticism arises from the recognition that we are just one small part of a much more extensive world. Our existence is contingent, a result of random mutation and natural selection; we occupy a particular and tiny region of space for an all too finite stretch of time; our knowledge is confined to what the world happens to offer to our sensitive surfaces and what our brains can interpret. Objectively considered, we are just limited biological creatures, constructing a view of what lies outside us on the basis of the fragmentary data that come our way. Once we absorb the fact that we are beings *in* the world, with certain restricted receptivities and powers, and with only those few pounds of neural meat to rely on, then we must wonder whether we are really in a position to form an objective picture of the world outside us. For why should that vast independent world yield up its secrets to squirming evolutionary parvenus such as ourselves? Is it not just luck if our brains allow us to form an accurate representation of the world as it exists independently of us? Is not our so-called knowledge bound to reflect our specific constitution, biological needs, subjective biases? Naturalistically considered, we are far from Godlike, epistemically and otherwise. Scepticism is thus the only realistic – the only *scientific* – attitude to adopt. Pretensions to objective knowledge are mere hubris, stemming from a reluctance to accept that we are nature's creatures – and not the other way about.

Both these lines of thought trade upon the idea that there is a metaphysical gap between the knower and what he or she aspires to know. In the first-person version the gap is between states of consciousness and conditions in the external world; in the third-person version the gap is conceived in terms of one part of the objective world being set over against another, each with its own intrinsic properties. These gaps are then held to have normative consequences, to the effect that we cannot properly *justify* what we are inclined to believe about what lies outside us. The philosophical problem of knowledge, then, is to show how the gaps in question may be bridged in such a way as to sustain our commonsense claims to knowledge. We have to show that knowledge is possible despite these gaps; that the gaps are not as destructive of knowledge as the sceptical line of thought suggests. This may, of course, take the form of showing that the alleged gaps are more apparent than real.

Let me remark some connections between this topic and our earlier discussions. First, a general point about philosophical perplexity and explanatory gaps: where we have the latter we tend to be visited with the former, at least when the gap attains a certain magnitude or quality. We have seen this repeatedly, as items we commonsensically take to be essentially related fall asunder as we try to articulate their connection: consciousness and the brain, selves and their attributes, meaning and use/training, free will and antecedent attitudes, a priori knowledge and its abstract objects, empirical knowledge and its grounds. Clearly there are important differences in the explanatory problems raised by these different cases, but what unites them is a certain opacity about the relations in question: the world appears to contain puzzling chasms, areas in which our initial sense of connectedness resists theoretical certification. Thus philosophy consists largely in fretting over such gaps, in exercises in bridge building – or denying that there is really anything on the other side (eliminativism). And part of the thrust of TN is to insist that these gaps are ultimately gaps in our understanding and are to be interpreted as such: no matter how profound the gap may appear to us, even to the point of necessary unbridgeability, it is always epistemological, not ontological, in origin. Something objective spans the gap; it is just that we cannot incorporate this into our scheme for making the world intelligible to ourselves (CALM regularly comes into this).

More specifically – and this is my second point – consciousness plays a key role in generating the first-person form of scepticism: the problem is how to get beyond one's current state of conscious awareness. This problem cannot but be shaped by our conception of the kind of thing consciousness is, and how it is related to other aspects of nature; in particular, its felt ontological autonomy is surely part of what powers the sceptical thought. And of course knowledge is, at least in its paradigm cases, itself a condition *of* consciousness.

Questions about the possibility of knowledge also intersect with questions about meaning, since both involve intentionality. We puzzle over our ability to know what lies outside us as we do over our ability to refer yonder. And there are well-recognized connections between our semantic capacities and our epistemic ones, some philosophers holding that the former are grounded in the latter.[2] The tendency to identify reference with 'knowledge of' is testament to this affinity. Thus problems about the possibility of meaning are bound to bear upon the possibility of knowledge, and contrariwise. Underdetermination problems, for example, are standard fare in both areas, leading to parallel sceptical anxieties.[3]

Less obviously, there is an abstract affinity between the problem of knowledge and the free will problem, especially where the acquisition of knowledge is concerned. In both cases we have sudden saltations or discontinuities, leading us to invoke mysterious faculties of creativity. From fragmentary data we generate a rich and integrated system of knowledge; from desire and other attitudes we leap to a free choice. In neither case is there any unique determination of the final state by the input values, at least of a kind we can comprehend; instead we have a looseness or freedom in the transition from one to the other, a qualitative shift to something of another order altogether. It is as if the mind moves into a higher gear – only we have no idea what the gear mechanism might look like. In view of this similarity, it is not surprising that the projection of theory from data is sometimes spoken of in terms of the notion of decision, as if only something like free choice could explain how we ascend from our paltry subjective inputs to the state of objective knowledge.

II DIME and Knowledge

Responses to the question of how knowledge is possible fall into the usual four categories. Domesticating theories attempt an explanatory account of how knowledge hooks up with the world, closing the gap that seemed to preclude knowledge. They may be divided into two groups, according as they focus on the knowledge relation or the thing known. The latter type of theory construes the world in such a fashion as to bring it epistemically closer to the knowing mind: phenomenalism and idealism thus interpret the world *as* mental in nature, so that no reaching outside the mind is really necessary in order to have knowledge of the world.[4] These theories are the strategic analogue of materialism about the mind as an answer to the question of the psychophysical link. The former type of theory, on the other hand, essays a sceptic-silencing story about the character of the knowledge relation, intended to render it perspicuous from a naturalistic standpoint. Thus it is suggested that knowledge consists in reliable correlation or nomological tracking or simple causation: these are the relations between belief and fact that constitute knowledge.[5] A recent variant of this approach invokes externalism about mental content to ensure that the mind and the world can never come apart in the radical way the sceptic envisages.[6] Knowledge is possible because our epistemic states are related thus-and-so to the world outside, where the relations in question infringe no naturalistic scruple.

Irreducibility proponents characteristically refuse to start on the explanatory path; they see no need to answer the sceptic with a *theory* of knowledge. What is needed, rather, is a diagnosis of the sceptic's neurosis, and a stubborn insistence on the inviolability of our ordinary practices. The word 'know' and its cognates have an established use, with conditions of justified assertion: to deny the applicability of these words is merely perverse linguistic legislation. The concept of knowledge *must* apply to the kinds of case that constitute its paradigm instances. I just *do* know that (e.g.) I have two hands, or that the earth has existed for over a hundred years.[7] If it is asked *how* I know, then nothing can be said save in the ordinary terms we bring to such questions – because I have looked, because that is what I have been taught. We have criteria for employing the word 'know', as we do for all other words, and when these are met no other question remains. Only semantic distortion and misplaced hyperbole could seem to undermine what we commonsensically know about knowledge. Our justifying practices are what they are; we make useful distinctions by appeal to them; our concepts are in order as they stand.

Historically, epistemological supernaturalism has featured prominently, with knowledge partaking of the divine. Plato set the tone, of course, with his doctrine of anamnesis and the ontology of the Forms;[8] but Descartes's system is the clearest expression of a divinely-based answer to scepticism, with knowledge secured by way of God's essential nature.[9] Our innate ideas are caused by God and it is God's non-deceptive nature that guarantees that we are not in massive error about the external world. Berkeley's system, likewise, makes God an essential cog in the epistemological machine.[10] On these conceptions, atheism is incompatible with knowledge, and only the special properties of the divine can offer a convincing answer to scepticism. Not for nothing is omniscience regarded as a defining feature of the Godlike: God's belief system is necessarily proof against any sceptical challenge. Subjection to error is the mark of the earthly, the human; true wisdom is what lifts us above this mortal coil. The prophet and the seer are revered because of the knowledge they possess, and this is what stamps them as divinely inspired. Perhaps part of our customary reverence for knowledge stems from these religious associations. In any case, there is a recognizable tradition, more or less philosophically systematic, that links knowing with Believing.

Outright scepticism is the form eliminativism takes in the case of knowledge: the sceptical challenge is succumbed to, and knowing declared impossible.[11] Our usual ascriptions of knowledge are groundlessly optimistic and naive, failing to take account of our true epistemic predicament – the fundamental distinction between our consciousness and the world beyond, our localized containment within an independent and indifferent reality. Once we review our position objectively we see that the concept of knowledge blithely ignores these facts, proceeding as if there were no real distinction between self and world – a stage common in the developing child and sometimes pathologically reverted to in later life. Since we might really be brains in vats, or be perpetually dreaming, or be systematic distorters of what enters through our senses, the only correct conclusion is that we do not know what we unthinkingly take ourselves to know. The concept of knowledge must therefore be eliminated or severely restricted, and some less demanding description of our epistemic powers devised. Once again, the E advocate says, the M theorist was onto something, namely that *only* a miracle could give us what we unreflectively demand: but since there are no miracles we must give up what could only be so on the assumption that there are. D theories fail to capture the full strength of what our ordinary notions require, and I doctrines simply fail to meet the sceptic's legitimate challenge; so it is either M or E – and extrusion is better than magic. We should learn to live without the comforting illusion that we know things.[12]

III   TN and Knowledge

Thomas Nagel writes: 'The idea of a full conception of reality that explains our ability to arrive at it is just a dream.'[13] To have a theory of knowledge is to have a theory of our theory-forming capacities; in the limit it would include a theory *of* that very theory. Such a theory would have two components: a theory of the objects of knowledge (the world), and a theory of human epistemic capacities – the two components being brought intelligibly together. This theory would explain how our cognitive states succeed in attaining the status of knowledge of the world; why the relation between the two is not merely accidental. If the theory is to vindicate our putative knowledge, then the naturalistic part of the theory must provide the basis for a normative reconstruction of what we believe: that is, the facts about the relation in question must be such as to yield, in conjunction with certain normative principles, a justification for what we commonsensically hold.[14] The question, then, so far as TN is concerned, is whether this meta-theory is in principle accessible to human enquirers, given their particular biases. Would its not being so help explain the appeal of scepticism and our chronic reflective insecurity about the ultimate basis of our ordinary beliefs? Is philosophical perplexity about the possibility of knowledge an artifact of cognitive closure with respect to the vindicating explanatory theory?

Let us first observe that there is no a priori reason to suppose that the efficacy of our first-order knowledge systems can be recapitulated at the level of meta-theory; indeed, a properly naturalistic view of our epistemic capacities would suggest the opposite. Consider our knowledge of language. Very plausibly, humans possess an innate module for language that enables them to develop linguistic abilities with remarkable ease and rapidity, despite the thin and degenerate character of the linguistic stimuli they receive. We are specifically designed to develop linguistic knowledge at a certain period of maturation; or better, we possess a particular faculty with that purpose. And this has a clear biological rationale – namely, quickly to confer the benefits of language, both cognitive and communicative, upon members of a highly reason-driven and social species. But from none of this does it follow, logically or empirically, that we should *also* have the capacity to understand, by the use of reason, the principles that enter into the formation of our (implicit) knowledge of language. It does not follow, that is, that the rational grammarian should be able to reconstruct what his innate language module achieved so readily. It is, on the contrary, entirely consistent to suppose that knowledge of language of the ordinary kind should coexist with principled theoretical ignorance of what constitutes and makes possible this knowledge. What we know as speakers might not be accessible to us as theorists.[15] And why should it be, since the biological advantages of explicit theoretical knowledge of language are moot at best? Once we adopt a modular view of linguistic knowledge, we shall regard meta-theoretical understanding as more a lucky accident than a natural by-product. Questions about the status of our first-order linguistic knowledge might then not be answerable by means of the exercise of our rational conscious faculties.

Much the same can be said about other components of our commonsense system of knowledge, notably knowledge of the external world and folk psychology. There is good reason to believe that these two cognitive areas are also innately based, modular, and special-purpose: they involve 'mental organs' that 'grow' under appropriate environmental conditions, with their own inner architecture and genesis, serving specific biological needs of the organism. Suppose this is so; then here are two specific knowledge modules whose inner principles and relations to the incoming data are potential subjects of theoretical enquiry. But, again, there is no particular reason to believe that our reflective capacities can penetrate the operations of these modules; no reason, that is, to think that we possess second-order knowledge capacities that are geared to understanding the achievements of our first-order faculties. What we need, as survival machines, is knowledge of how the physical world and other sentient beings are apt to behave; nothing ensures, however, that we should be capable of knowledge of how we acquire such knowledge. It might simply be confusing for us to take on the additional burden of grasping how the world interacts with our faculties in such a way as to yield knowledge of that world. After all, we do not expect other cognitive animals to be epistemologists as well as knowers. TN is clearly the correct theory for canine knowledge (say): the dog knows but it cannot know how it knows.[16]

So there should be no presumption that we can arrive at the correct theory of how we come to know things. That theory might be accessible to Martians but not to us, with the attendant perplexity in our case and complacency in theirs. They might then sympathize with our epistemic insecurities while seeing that there is no objective basis for them; they understand why we are prone to sceptical anxieties, given the poverty of our reflective epistemology, but they also see that these anxieties are groundless. For them it is obvious that we humans do indeed know what we naively take ourselves to know; but they also find it intelligible that we cannot appreciate this fact at a theoretical level. That is just the way we are cognitively structured, epistemically speaking.

This sounds like a liberating possibility, if a somewhat chastening one, but can it be made plausible? I shall approach this question in three parts: first, by comparing TN about knowledge with the DIME options; second, by trying to identify specific aspects of our epistemological perplexity that are suggestive of TN; third, by asking whether there is anything that positively precludes blocking scepticism by invoking TN.

Clearly, part of the appeal of TN depends here, as always, on the relative attractiveness of the other available alternatives. Clearly, too, there is at least as much dissension and partisanship in epistemology as in the other philosophical areas we have touched upon; aside perhaps from the M option, representatives of each of the remaining three schools (DIE) are to be found lurking in some corridor or other. As hitherto, I shall not undertake a critique of each of the many positions that have been advocated; I speak for those who are dissatisfied with the standard approaches and suspect the workings of a flawed presupposition – or are just interested in what other approach might be considered. Let me then record my conviction that D theories systematically fail to answer the core of the sceptical challenge; that I doctrines simply ignore the genuine force of scepticism; that M creeds are false where they achieve conceptual coherence; that E conclusions are sufficiently alarming and counterintuitive to be treated only as a last resort. In sum, I say, scepticism is irrefutable by any of the standard moves, or conceivable variants on them, but it is also unacceptable as an actual response to the corrosive power of the considerations that seem to prompt it. So we should look with considerable favour upon any approach that promises to release us from this familiar bind. What TN says, in brief, is that the resources for a successful rebuttal of scepticism exist only in a theory whose content is inaccessible to human cognition. Thus we are actually right to cleave to our ordinary knowledge claims, despite our principled inability to reply to sceptical doubts. We are prey to scepticism and kindred epistemological anxieties precisely because we cannot grasp the explanatory theory that would lay our scepticism to rest – the theory that spells out exactly how our cognitive states relate to the world of which they purport to provide knowledge. We cannot know the theory that certifies our knowledge, but we can have the knowledge thus objectively certified. So TN says that scepticism is false but unknowably so: that is the root of our philosophical difficulties about knowledge. TN allows us to stick with common sense without being forced to adopt implausible and distorting philosophical theories. Therein lies its advantage over the DIME options.

In the nature of the case, establishing TN is largely so much fumbling in the dark, but we can sometimes detect pockets of particular incomprehensibility that are at least suggestive of the truth of TN – recurring themes, uncashable metaphors. So it is with the case of knowledge. I would locate the recalcitrant core of scepticism in two problematic notions: that of what conscious awareness can contain, and that of the rationality of our modes of inference. The former notion relates to the potential constituency of conscious experience, the items with which it acquaints us: are these ever objects from the extra-mental world? And the difficulty lies in understanding how conscious states succeed in reaching out to the external facts and embracing them in such a way as to make us genuinely acquainted with them. This is of course strongly reminiscent of the problem of reference or intentionality, but it should also remind us of the mind–body problem – in that in both cases we have trouble grasping the nature of a linkage that cannot be regarded as purely contingent or extrinsic. Here we confront a cluster of problems centering on the difficulty of intelligibly relating conscious states to other items in the world, where the relation needs to be of a particularly strong form in order to secure what we want – a reply to scepticism and a solution to the mind–body problem. One aspect of our epistemological perplexity, then, traces back to the theoretical impenetrability of consciousness: we do not understand what kind of relation could bind experience to the world in the way we assume that it does when we speak of knowledge. What *is* it for my mind to project outward into the world, so giving me (a self) acquaintance with things? What kind of mechanism or process could account for the requisite internality of this relation?[17] We draw a blank here, and so fail to provide a theory that would explain what the sceptic questions. The epistemic powers of the mind thus come to seem entirely inwardly directed, with an unbridgeable gulf opening up between awareness and the external world. According to TN, however, this retreat inwards results from an illusion borne of cognitive closure with respect to the epistemic powers of consciousness.[18] Consciousness really does acquaint us, in the fullest sense, with things outside the mind, but it does so in virtue of an essential nature we cannot comprehend – just as it emerges naturally from the brain in virtue of such a hidden nature. The ultimate source of this aspect of scepticism thus lies in our inability to provide a proper theory of the nature of consciousness.

The second problematic notion that nourishes scepticism is that of rational inference; and this problem is most acute when the inference is abductive or 'nondemonstrative'. When the premisses for an inference fail logically to entail the conclusion drawn we worry over problems of evidential underdetermination: other conclusions seem compatible with the evidence, so what warrants deriving one conclusion rather than another? Often enough, we take a certain conclusion to be the intuitively correct one, the others being artificially manufactured to make a philosophical point.[19] Here then we find exemplified the classic form of a philosophical puzzle – an unexplained transition from one kind of thing to another, with no clear principles available to sustain the leap. Naturally enough, we find talk of novelty and creativity at this point, of inspiration and intuition, of the mind being no mere algorithmic machine. But such talk is of little help against scepticism, which wonders what rational basis there could be for the inferences we ordinarily make. Who is to say that the mind is not just firing off according to its own prejudices, preferring one conclusion over the others for no good reason? What *grounds* are there to think that our abductive propensities are geared to track the truth? Unless such grounds can be supplied it looks as if the output of our reasoning faculties cannot rank as knowledge.

TN views the sceptical problem about rational inference as follows. First, it notes the tell-tale invocation of promissory notions like novelty and inferential 'quantum leaps': these notions signal an area of deep theoretical blankness, a fundamental incapacity to expose the operative principles – as they do in other areas we have discussed. Secondly, TN offers the conjecture that the certifying principles of abductive inference are not accessible to us, save as implicitly controlling our knowledge-acquiring procedures. We are in fact subject to principles that make our inferences rationally warranted but we cannot properly articulate what those principles are – though we can, to be sure, make more or less inadequate shots at the task.[20] Our beliefs are indeed systematically sensitive to the facts, thus counting as genuine knowledge, but we are at a loss to detail what this sensitivity consists in. We might be compared, in this respect, with other animals whose belief systems likewise home in, quite naturally, on a certain view of the world, but whose ability to reconstruct the principles that govern the formation of their beliefs is virtually non-existent. The dog rationally believes its master is home when its senses are bombarded thus-and-so, but it is quite unable to give any account of why this is the rational conclusion to draw as opposed to some other; indeed, it might not be capable of meta-beliefs at all. The dog can say or think nothing that even begins to quell the sceptic's doubts about what it spontaneously believes, but it does not follow that those doubts *have* no answer. Similarly, our inability explicitly to demonstrate the rationality of our beliefs, be it never so terminal, does not imply that no principles *exist* that would provide the needed demonstration. Those clever Martians might have the principles well in hand, so seeing that our natural modes of inference are the right ones – but also that we are not up to appreciating this at a reflective level. In other words, we might be a lot more rational than we can ever recognize reflectively, on account of our principled inability to understand the operations of our abductive faculties. The sceptic, on this hypothesis, is misconstruing a deep meta-theoretical lack as a case of ground-floor unreason: but it does not follow from the fact that we cannot explicitly grasp or articulate the rationality of human reason that it is anything short of fully rational. That would be like deducing from our theoretical inability to provide a grammar for human languages that the language faculty itself contains no such grammar. Our speech may be grammatically governed, at an implicit level, without it being possible for us to articulate consciously what the underlying grammatical principles are. TN sees in the durability of scepticism about inference the operation of cognitive closure with respect to the nature of our inferential faculties.

The third point I said I would address concerns the internal viability of our epistemic practices: is there anything in the way we form our beliefs that reveals them to be inherently irrational? For if there is, then we are facing something a good deal more radical than the mere *lack* of an explicit rationale for what we believe; and TN can only perform its healing work in this latter kind of case, not the former. We need, that is, to assure ourselves that the sceptic has no valid proof of the *im*possibility of knowledge. Fear that our inferential practices can be shown to be inherently irrational is likely to stem from the admitted transcendence of theory over data: this in itself, it might be said, already shows that what we naturally infer cannot count as knowledge. But the inferential gap here does not by itself undermine knowledge, unless it implies something knowledge-destroying about the relation between belief and fact – that this relation is merely accidental or serendipitous or some such. And this latter claim is what TN questions: principles beyond our grasp determine our beliefs as not merely true by luck, but as (when true) true by virtue of knowledge-constituting links to the world. So the sceptic cannot rely on the mere appearance of contingency or luck to argue that our knowledge claims are unwarranted, since this appearance might well be belied by the underlying mechanisms and processes that produce our beliefs. The link between belief and fact might be much more finely tuned and internal than our own conception of our knowledge suggests.[21] As ever, we must be careful not to confuse the absence of a theory of something with the presence of a theory that denies that thing.

Analytic philosophy of knowledge has proceeded on the assumption that scepticism is to be refuted, if it can be, from within our given scheme of epistemic concepts, by dissecting the notions of justification and inference and so forth that we possess. This approach has not, I venture to suggest, succeeded, the sceptical problem simply looking more severe the clearer we become about our concepts. We cannot, it begins to seem, construct a theory that shows how knowledge is possible just by staying within the set of concepts we bring to our cognitive activities. TN interprets this failure as a mark in its favour: for the falsity of scepticism is only evident, it holds, from outside our system of concepts, by consulting a theory that transcends our powers of comprehension. This ideal theory contains, in particular, an explanation of the powers of consciousness and an articulation of the principles governing our abductive faculties – the lack of both of which lies at the heart of our sceptical problems. It is a chapter of human psychology that we ourselves are unequipped to write but which explains one of our psychological achievements: our ability to know things about the world outside us. The objective existence of this theory is what secures the possibility (and frequency) of human knowledge.

Let me end this chapter with a disclaimer. Knowledge is a complex and polymorphous phenomenon, covering many different domains and bodies of organizing principle. Sceptical doubts about its feasibility are likewise various and multiply motivated. I have been speaking in a very general way about what I take to constitute the intractable pith of philosophical perplexity about the possibility of knowledge, particularly in relation to knowledge of material objects. I do not mean to suggest that every epistemological problem should or could be treated in the TN style, nor that all forms of scepticism require appeal to transcendent facts to diagnose or resolve them. Some epistemological problems may well be soluble by means of conceptual analysis, or indeed by human empirical science. What I have wanted to suggest is that there is a basic core to the problem that can be brought under the general framework provided by TN; an area of theoretical mystery that forms the root of our philosophical difficulties. This is the remarkable capacity of the mind radically to transcend the input received, projecting a richly structured representation of the outside world, which nevertheless is sufficiently intimately connected to that world that its states count as genuine knowledge – which, indeed, manages to incorporate the world into its own inner landscape. Somehow the mind contrives to make cognitive contact with the facts, despite their apparent remoteness from the processes that mediate this contact. The sceptic denies that there really is any such knowledge-constituting contact, because of the paucity and frailty of the intervening processes; TN counters this by suggesting that our conception of these processes might be extremely limited, so that the full story would dissolve our puzzlement about the putative mental contact, if only it were accessible to us. Knowledge only *seems* philosophically problematic, because we are so far away from grasping its objective enabling conditions. In fact, our commonsense knowledge is as inherently robust and unqualified as we naively suppose; it is just that we are blocked from arriving at the theory that explains why this is so. Scepticism perenially afflicts us because of this latter fact, not because our knowledge claims themselves are intrinsically suspect or shaky.

NOTES

1   For treatments sympathetic to scepticism, see Barry Stroud, *The Significance of Philosophical Scepticism*, and Thomas Nagel, *The View From Nowhere*, chapter 5.
2   Russell bases reference on acquaintance, which is a type of knowledge: see *The Problems of Philosophy*, chapter 5. Gareth Evans follows Russell in this, making discriminating knowledge the foundation of reference: see *The Varieties of Reference*.
3   Thus the only possible grounds for the reference relation are held to be insufficient to determine a unique assignment of reference, while the reasons for our knowledge claims are likewise held to be compatible with a range of epistemic alternatives. Both reference and knowledge are taken to exceed the 'input', thus presenting problems of possibility.
4   Berkeley explicitly tailors the nature of reality to conform to the principle that only what is in the mind can be known: see *A Treatise Concerning the Principles of Human Knowledge*. Given that principle, scepticism will follow from anything other than idealism about the objects of knowledge.
5   See Robert Nozick, *Philosophical Explanations*, chapter 3.

6 See Hilary Putnam, *Reason, Truth and History*, chapter 1; Donald Davidson, 'A Coherence Theory of Truth and Knowledge'. I discuss this approach, sceptically, in *Mental Content*, chapter 1.

7 See G. E. Moore, 'Proof of an External World'; Wittgenstein, *On Certainty*.

8 Plato, *The Republic*.

9 Descartes, *Meditations*.

10 Berkeley, *A Treatise Concerning the Principles of Human Knowledge*.

11 See Peter Unger, *Ignorance: a Case for Scepticism*.

12 The concept of certainty plays a key role in the debate about knowledge: for it is the difficulty of securing certainty (without reliance upon God) that leads most directly to scepticism. In the text I have formulated the sceptical problem in terms of the concept of knowledge, but I could have spoken of certainty and justification instead; nothing crucial turns on my focus on knowledge.

13 *The View From Nowhere*, p. 85.

14 It is worth noting explicitly that a solution to the naturalistic aspect of the problem of knowledge would not automatically yield a solution to the normative aspect of the problem. For we might be able to develop a full theory of the natural basis of the mind's capacity to generate rich systems of belief without this vindicating the applicability of normative notions like knowledge and justification to our beliefs. TN with respect to knowledge might then operate at a purely normative level: we might fail to comprehend by what normative principles the totality of natural facts underlying our beliefs could generate knowledge properly so called. We might, that is, grasp how we in fact come to have our beliefs but be closed to what justifies them. However, the natural facts cannot fail to have some bearing on the question of justification.

15 The general principle here is that the internal structure proper to a faculty F1 might not be replicable by a distinct faculty F2 – a principle that is obviously correct for bodily organs. Of course, we do know a good deal, by means of the faculty of reason, about the internal structure of the language faculty; my point in the text is a purely theoretical one. I think our relative success in this area has to do with the syntactic or formal character of the contents of the language faculty. Other types of knowledge, in which consciousness and reasoning play an essential part, raise problems of a different order. Grammatical representation might thus be explicable by human reason without this implying that other kinds of knowledge are. Scepticism has not been supposed to apply to our mastery

of grammar, while our empirical knowledge – which purports to take us beyond ourselves – has seemed far more problematic. The deep differences between these sorts of knowledge (or representation) make any move from the comprehensibility of one sort to that of others suspect. Our conscious rational faculty might be a mystery to itself while our grammatical faculty is a mere problem – despite the fact that the word 'know' can be used for the output of both sorts of faculty. If so, the nature of the language faculty is not representative of other knowledge systems we possess.

16   We cannot assume that we are superior to the dog in this respect because we can do science and the dog cannot, since there is no guarantee that our scientific faculties are equipped to grasp what makes knowledge possible – even the knowledge of a dog.

17   Causal relations between the environment and the brain are often invoked at this point, but it is hard to feel satisfied with this because such relations are scarcely specific to knowledge. No account of the encompassing power of conscious awareness issues from these kinds of causal relations – which is why a causal perspective of this sort is often thought to lead to scepticism.

18   This aspect of scepticism has been neglected in recent epistemology, because consciousness itself has been a neglected topic; but traditional discussions were expressly concerned with the question of the proper objects of consciousness. A central epistemological issue has been whether consciousness can present items that are ontologically independent of itself – a question that clearly depends upon some understanding of the nature and powers of consciousness. To discuss scepticism without considering consciousness is to ignore an essential aspect of the problem.

19   As with the brain in the vat hypothesis, or Nelson Goodman's 'grue': see *Fact, Fiction and Forecast*.

20   We have, if you like, implicit mastery of the rules of inference that would, if they could be made explicit, silence the sceptic. Our conscious knowledge rests upon a subconscious mastery of justificatory principles – in somewhat the way our knowledge of what people say rests upon a subconscious mastery of grammar. TN about knowledge is thus the idea that this mastery is necessarily implicit: we cannot reconstruct the implicated principles by means of conscious reason – hence sceptical anxieties at a reflective level.

21   Compare a child's deductively derived knowledge: she reasons in accordance with logical principles but she cannot state those principles or even recognize their correctness when put to her. In this position, then, she might be forgiven for entertaining sceptical doubts

about the knowledge she derives by deductive inference, but in fact there are principles (deductive logic) that would adequately rebut such doubts. Just as people reasoned validly before Aristotle discovered syllogistic logic, so we might now be reasoning validly in non-deductive contexts though no one *could* ever discover the underlying certifying principles. From the fact that we cannot consciously know what justifies our knowledge it does not follow that nothing does; so scepticism, though understandable, might yet be objectively false.

8

Reason, Truth and Philosophy

I Biology and Reason

Think of the human being as a vertebrate congeries of disparate organs, both bodily and psychological. Each of these organs has its own function, structure, implementation, principles of operation. Each performs its specific task in virtue of these constitutive characteristics, more or less successfully; certain effects are brought about as a result of causative factors within them, identified at the appropriate level of description. These organs exhibit task limitations of various sorts, concerning surrounding conditions of smooth functioning, stress levels, fatigue patterns, capacity bounds – all the factors that determine what they can achieve and when. They are also subject to disease, damage, pathology, luck. They are natural objects in a natural world, heir to the frailties that beset such objects. Among these mortal organs are some that traffic in information, that have their effects as a result of representations they contain (there is controversy about which organs are thus informaton-driven); their task description accordingly involves mention of their informational powers and limitatons. And among these semantic organs are those that implicate consciousness in their operations – those in which conscious states appear to play a task-relevant role. Chief among these is the organ we call 'reason' – which no doubt itself decomposes into a number of sub-organs or systems. At a first level of approximation, we can characterize it as the organ by means of which we form conscious beliefs, on the basis of evidence, about a wide variety of subject matters; in particular, it is the organ responsible for what we think of as our theoretical knowledge of the world. We use it, among other things, for doing philosophy: it is the organ deployed in the search for the kind of truth proper to that designation. Not the heart or the kidneys, nor yet the senses of sight or touch: when the task is philosophy the organ we bring to bear is our capacity to form beliefs as a result of reasoning – we expect reason to deliver philosophical truths as its output, represented in the form of conscious thoughts.

This may sound like a banal observation, but actually it conceals a substantive and disputable assumption, namely that the organ we call 'reason' is inherently suited to the production of philosophical truth. Put differently, it is the assumption that the phenomena of traditional interest to philosophers – for example, those discussed in the last six chapters – have natures that are susceptible to investigation by means of human reason and its adjoining organs. And the essential point is that this assumption is by no means necessarily or trivially true. It is a factual empirical claim about a certain human faculty and a certain domain of truth. For, unless we think of philosophical truth as *created* by human reason, the question must arise as to how good that faculty is as a means of gaining insight into the objective phenomena of interest to us; and we must approach this question in an impartial and open-minded spirit, sensitive to the evidence we have about the powers of this organ in that domain and to the broader principles governing the scope and limits of human faculties. It is a question of the same general order as whether the belief system of the dog or the orangutan or the human five-year-old or the autistic adult is capable of ascertaining the kind of truth sought by philosophers. Or again (even more tendentiously) it is like asking whether conscious reason is the appropriate organ to use in the acquisition of language, as opposed to the subconscious language module; or whether, unaided, it is a good way to ascertain the spatial layout of objects in one's immediate environment, as opposed to using the organ of sight. The question then, starkly put, is whether a naturalistic view of human reason supports the empirical assumption that the kinds of phenomena discussed in previous chapters are susceptible of understanding by the use of that particular human organ. Are human reason and philosophical truth cut out for one another?

I have been arguing, in effect, for a negative answer to that question, by way of a piecemeal discussion of particular topics; now I want to tackle the question more directly and generally, focusing upon the specific properties of the reasoning faculty. Since our understanding of this faculty is itself extremely limited what I shall have to say must perforce be highly speculative, and it is entirely in keeping with the drift of this book to acknowledge that we might never be able to comprehend the workings of reason – including what it is constitutionally blind to. Still, we might be able to gain some general sense of why reason seems, as suggested earlier, to be so inept at answering the philosophical questions it so readily poses to itself; at any rate, I propose in this chapter to speculate, somewhat brutally, on the question.

It cannot, I just said, be simply taken for granted that the human reasoning faculty is naturally suited for answering philosophical questions: the questions and their subject-matter are one thing; the rational faculty, as a human trait, is another. From the fact that it is the best faculty we have (but see below) for doing philosophy it does not follow that it is a remotely good or adequate faculty for that purpose. In the case of a person born with damage to their innate language centre reason may be the best means they have available for learning a natural language, but this means might be faltering at best and defective at critical junctures. Such a module-deficient person may laboriously apply their conscious reasoning faculties to the task, making slow progress, coming up against areas of impenetrable mystery, much like a scientific linguist trying to articulate an explicit theory, perhaps not even realizing that other faculties are conceivable that can master these problems far more rapidly and smoothly. In humans the acquisition of language is not what reason is *for*; that task is allotted to a special-purpose language faculty, equipped with its own architecture and *modus operandi*. Thus we might say that the truths of grammar are naturally targeted by that specific faculty, and may or may not be accessible to the reasoning faculty. In much the same way, I am suggesting, the truths of philosophy – that is, the correct theory of the phenomena discussed earlier – might not lie in the target area of reason; or might do so only at the far fringes of its efficient operation, not yet so much as glimpsed; or only by means of intellectual prostheses; or only after substantial cerebral enhancement – at any rate, not reason as it is now constituted. And this counter-philosophical blindness or bias is what produces the sense of peculiar depth we experience when doing philosophy, not anything intrinsic to the facts contemplated. A flat reality is interpreted as having anomalous bumps as a result of our own cognitive deficits. We are like selective dyslexics trying to read the Book of Nature: some letter combinations pose no difficulty, while others constantly trip us up. But we tend not to see it that way, preferring to find some special potency, or defect, in the illegible combinations. Perhaps only the discovery of a race of 'normal readers', those to whom philosophical questions have straightforward answers, could ever fully convince us of the true nature of our predicament; or, better for our vanity, the discovery of cognitive creatures with reading abilities that are inverted relative to ours – their intellectual contortions over simple mechanics might be a useful lesson to us, compensating for the philosophical humiliations they laughingly inflict on our species.[1]

To give this idea colour, clearly, we need to identify properties of the reasoning faculty that produce the kind of selective (in)competence TN diagnoses; a litany of failures is not enough, suggestive as it may be. To this end, I earlier introduced the CALM conjecture, a hypothesis about the kinds of content naturally accessible to our reasoning faculties. In a nutshell, the suggestion was that when we can apply this form of explanatory scheme to some domain we produce intellectually satisfying results, in which problems are solved and intelligibility is high – but otherwise not. CALM theories are the natural inhabitants of our human cognitive space. If we can treat a given domain as made up of primitive elements that combine according to stateable laws or rules to produce complex results, then we achieve a state of explanatory equilibrium. In particular, kinds of 'novelty' that can be explained in this way are rendered unmysterious: new formations of matter, both organic and inorganic, derived by material rearrangement; new mathematical structures got by successive iterations of specified operations; new sentences that have never been produced before generated from a fixed base of grammatical rules. So it goes with the physical sciences, with biology, with mathematics, with syntax: these are all CALM-able domains. Quite possibly, it is the fundamentally spatial nature of our modes of awareness that lies behind our adroitness with CALM structures; the rest comes from extensions and modifications of this of one kind or another. The geometrical mode of thought is the one that is natural to our species: *homo geometricus*, as we might say.[2]

But, the conjecture goes, this mode of understanding is brought up short when it comes to handling the kinds of question discussed earlier. The entities and relations that prompt philosophical perplexity are not construable in the CALM style. Thus, to summarize: consciousness is not a combinatorial emergent with respect to brain constituents; the self is likewise not related in this kind of way to bodily and mental characteristics; meaning is not a mere complex of the facts that form its supervenience base; free choices are not just vectors of prior states and events; the relation between a priori knowledge and its objects is not that of a lawlike mapping within a unitary space of elements; empirical knowledge transcends the grounds on which we base it and is not simply a rearrangement of them. Notions of novelty and underdetermination are endemic to these areas, but these notions are not explicable according to the CALM paradigm – as purely combinatorial novelty. There is a pervasive impression that nature is conjuring something from nothing, or from not enough, as if it could construct things from demonstrably inadequate materials with no intelligible plan. According to TN, however, this cannot really be how nature goes about its business, but it will seem to us that it works this way because we cannot formulate the requisite theories; and the CALM conjecture says that we cannot do so because we cannot bring the phenomena under the combinatorial mode of understanding with which we naturally operate. Hence the epistemological discontinuity between the sciences and philosophy. Human reason is inherently CALM, at least where it can produce deep natural knowledge; but philosophical problems characteristically resist the CALM treatment, so baffling us through and through.

There may be a connection between the CALM conjecture and a further property of reason, namely its link to consciousness, if it is true that *conscious* representations are what inherently conform to the CALM format – a question we shall come to presently. But in any case it is worth dwelling upon this property of reason, as it suggests limitations on its own account: being conscious itself appears to impose intrinsic capacity constraints upon the operations of reason. It may then be that reason cannot solve the problem of consciousness (*inter alia*) precisely because it *is* conscious. So what are these constraints, and why does consciousness impose them? First, conscious activity is notoriously serial in its mode of operation: it cannot therefore handle much at the same time. This limits its processing capacity, requiring it to neglect what does not fall within the narrow field of attention. We can only concentrate on one problem at a time, more or less. While the brain itself engages in massively parallel informational activity, conscious reason plods serially through its tasks.[3] Second, conscious reasoning is remarkably slow, in addition to being one-tracked. Computers can perform equivalent tasks at a much faster rate, as witness those computer proofs of mathematical theorems that would take human reason decades to execute, and our sensory systems work far more rapidly than our belief system does.[4] Third, conscious reason is closely tied to our primary modes of awareness of the world, reflecting their specific character; it cannot stray too far from how the world appears to us, losing its grip if required to contravene the appearances. The conceptual and the experiential are intertwined, so that reason cannot operate as an independent system, wholly free of sensory awareness.[5] This seems to result from the fact that reason and sense share the same representational medium, namely consciousness. The pervasive spatiality of our conceptions reflects this link between reason and sense.[6] Thus, taken together, conscious reason is serial, slow and sensory (and hence spatial) – none of these properties being necessary features of any possible informational system. And these limits may well preclude reason from successfully solving problems that it can nevertheless appreciate.

A good way to gauge what a system can do is to ask what it was designed to do. In the case of machines we look at the intentions and plans of the designer; in the case of evolved organs we must look at the biological function of the organ, how it aids the organism's survival. Of course, things can often do more (or less) than they were designed to do, and there are sometimes by-products of the original design; but purpose is still a useful guide to power. So let us ask, in this biological spirit, what the reasoning organ of man is designed for. Note, to begin with, that reason is quite rare in the evolved world; most organisms get by without it. Rational belief formation is by no means a precondition of biological success; indeed, its disadvantages might, in the fullness of time, be seen to outweigh its advantages, leaving the planet to reasonless insects and the like.[7] We pride ourselves on that sudden explosion of the frontal lobes on which our reasoning capacity depends, but what is the basic biological point of it? What is the reproductive payoff of the capacity to form conscious beliefs? I think the answer can be stated in one word: flexibility. Forming beliefs may be laborious, energy-consuming and neurosis-producing, but the good thing about beliefs is that they can be changed if circumstances warrant it. Your store of beliefs is not a fixed hard-wired fact about you, unlike your anatomical structure or instinctive reflexes. Belief states are labile, shifting, plastic; they come and go, waxing and waning in strength, being constantly revised and updated. And given that these states are central causative factors in controlling human behaviour, they enable us to modify our behaviour in ways that other animals cannot. What is called 'culture' is a reflection of the plasticity of belief, combined with its causal efficacy. Another word for the same phenomenon is 'learning': not having to know everything in advance, and so not being hostage to changing circumstances. You only have to watch a fly trying to negotiate a pane of glass to appreciate the power of learning as against instinct. Or again, our own proneness to visual illusions that are impervious to knowledge of the true nature of the stimulus illustrates the perils of the fixed and ineducable.[8] Once the organism's environment changes the old hard-wired ways are no longer adaptive; one then needs the flexibility conferred by reason. The trade-off, as it seems to be, between speed and flexibility can seem more than worth it when events turn unpredictable. Reason is the organ whose speciality is change, and it is constructed accordingly.

I take it these remarks will seem reassuringly truistic. In the light of TN, however, they take on a more disturbing significance. For, if reason is designed with flexibility primarily in mind – itself a worthy biological aim – the question must arise as to whether it possesses the kinds of characteristics needed to generate the sort of knowledge we seek in philosophy. Why should a talent for (mere) flexibility be a sound basis for deep objective knowledge? Why should plastic representations inevitably be omniscient ones? Why should this functional feature of belief states correlate with extensiveness of objective coverage? There is no natural transition from the mere lability of belief to its being capable of the kinds of content needed to supply answers to philosophical questions; these are simply orthogonal dimensions along which representational systems can vary. A system might be highly labile in what it holds yet very narrow in the range of contents it can represent; or it might, conversely, be eternally fixed in what it holds and yet cover a wide range of heterogeneous contents. Strength along one dimension does not imply strength along the other; indeed, given the biological realities, systems must typically sacrifice one type of strength for another.[9]

There is a standard position on the question of how reason can achieve more, cognitively speaking, than seems extractable from its biological function. Philistine practicality, flexibly exercised, would seem to be what pure biology predicts – being educable in matters of feeding, fighting and mating. But that is not of course what we actually find: we find science, mathematics, art, philosophy – all going well beyond what reason *ought* to be expending its precious energies on. Why? Answer: these are all by-products of a faculty built with other purposes in view. Once you equip a creature with the capacity to think it is bound to think of other things than you originally intended. Intelligence spreads, even into areas in which it will do us no good. Scientific knowledge, then, is the rational faculty spinning idly on its biological axis, generating beliefs that have no reproductive rationale in themselves. And if science can come about in this derivative and unforseen way, then why not philosophy? True, reason was not designed with philosophical knowledge expressly in view, but what it was designed for contains the materials to lead, perhaps inevitably, to such knowledge. So it might be thought.

It seems to me that this line of reflection is much too sanguine. First, we should be a good deal more surprised by the by-product story than we tend to be, regarding it as far more puzzling than is customary. It really is quite astonishing, and not at all predictable, that a faculty with the biological function of reason should be capable of the feats of which it is capable. These are so biologically exceptional, and often so counter to our survival requirements, that it is a major puzzle why the genes did not at least install a mechanism to limit the exercise of reason in biologically desirable ways. Can it really be a necessary truth that you cannot have the biological benefits of reason, strictly defined, without also having quantum physics, surrealism and the transcendental deduction? Why do we not contain a blocking mechanism that inhibits us from abusing our reason in these ways? Is it that a few more million years of evolution will correct this error, creating people whose reason is less divagatory and distracting? If these are the by-products of human reason, then it looks like reason was designed, sloppily, without regard to the mental pollution it might produce.[10] We should certainly be surprised if some other species were to develop the kinds of abstract interests we have, given the concentration on survival we expect from them.

Secondly, if we take the by-product idea seriously we should be prepared to encounter limitations that derive from the primary purpose of the organ – as we would be for any other biological organ. The inner nature of reason, as determined by its basic function, must to some degree constrain the kinds of side-effects it can have. If we knew, for instance, that a given creature's reasoning faculty was designed solely in order to enable it more flexibly to negotiate the underground tunnels it blindly inhabits, with the contents of its practical beliefs limited to its given narrow environment, then we would be very sceptical of the suggestion that this faculty also confers on the creature – epiphenomenally, as it were – the ability to understand (say) the lives and environments of creatures that fly or swim, let alone yield philosophical knowledge of the kind we seek. We would need to be persuaded of some kind of conceptual or theoretical *continuity* if were to take the by-product suggestion seriously. Similarly, in our own case, the claim that philosophical knowledge can be expected as a by-product of our reason is just so much hand-waving until it is shown why human reason *should* extend in this direction. At least in the case of the physical sciences we can, though sketchily, tell a story about how our matter-in-space awareness might be extensible into more theoretical regions, the basic concepts and principles being refined and systematized. But nothing like this seems available as an account of how we could come to grasp the relevant theories for the phenomena discussed earlier in this book; these phenomena seem of a different order from anything encompassable in that way.[11] Nor, apparently, is a representation of their underlying nature accessible from our original naive conception of them in folk psychology. So without any bridge of theoretical continuity talk of philosophical knowledge as an intellectual by-product is empty. The onus is really on the defender of the by-product account of the possibility of philosophical knowledge to give some positive reason to believe this; antecedently, the more likely hypothesis, from a biological point of view, is that human reason is neither equipped for, nor aimed at, understanding the range of natural phenomena that occasion philosophical perplexity. The genes constructed human reason without so much as a thought to the philosophical powers of the species. And if they had thought of it, they would probably have built us in such a way as to prevent us even raising philosophical questions. They wanted practical flexibility from reason first and foremost, not philosophical insight into arcane matters. What should be surprising is that we know as much as we do, not that we do not know about things we would like to know about. The first dogma of Rationalism (in one sense of the term) is that human reason is intrinsically designed to penetrate to the objective nature of every part of reality.[12]

II Epistemic Pluralism

To say that human reason cannot solve a certain class of problems is not to say that nothing can. I now want to ask whether the class of philosophical problems might be soluble by some other faculty than reason; and I do not mean some merely possible fantasy faculty, stipulatively introduced, but rather an actually existing faculty with which we are more or less familiar. Are the answers to philosophical problems perhaps already represented at some other cognitive locale? My suggestion will be that, surprisingly enough, this is in fact quite likely, so that reason comes lower on the scale of cognitive achievement than we have tended to suppose. To see this, however, may require some major realignments of view.

I am going to assume that representational properties are not unique to conscious beliefs, that semantic predicates can apply, quite literally, to configurations of other sorts. I know of no good argument against this assumption and I think it is written into much successful theory; in any case, I shall not be undertaking to argue for it fully here.[13] This assumption – in effect, that representational content is not unique to reason – allows us to envisage the possibility of a comparative epistemology, in which the epistemic powers and properties of different systems are compared and evaluated. We have a genus consisting of systems that have syntactic and referential properties and then a number of species in which this broad natural kind is specialized into systems differing along other dimensions. We can then ask which systems are better suited for which cognitive tasks, according to their particular strengths and weaknesses. This kind of question can be asked about the faculties of different animal species, comparing their respective sensory capacities, memory limitations, learning potential. It can also be asked with respect to the several representational systems possessed by a given individual, human or other. Thus we can compare the faculties of (say) vision, language and reason in humans, enquiring into the kinds of content and processing principles that apply in each case – and there are developed theories that attempt to answer these questions. A commonly accepted principle here is that the various faculties employ semantic primitives of different kinds: the language faculty represents grammatical properties, themselves not normally represented at the level of conscious belief, while the visual faculty deals in features of presented arrays analysed so as to facilitate computations of the distal layout.[14] The systems differ in their expressive powers, in their functions, in their fixity, in their connections to behaviour, and so forth. Nobody would think that any one of them was necessarily equipped to do the job nature has assigned the others – that, say, the visual system could be used to learn language. There is a ranking here in terms of suitability to perform a given cognitive task. And reason does not come out on top with respect to every task: it may not, for example, be able to duplicate the representational capacities of the language faculty, so that the theoretical linguist is unable to make explicit what his language faculty implicitly or unconsciously contains already. In general, once we have accepted epistemic pluralism we cannot expect that reason will always be as capable, semantically or theoretically, as other representational systems we could mention. It is simply one system among many, with its own purposes and limitations, its own domain of efficient operation.[15]

Now I have argued that human reason is not suited to solving philosophical problems; but, given epistemic pluralism, it does not follow that *nothing* in human nature is so suited. It would be quite consistent with TN about philosophy and human reason to hold that some other semantic system within us has *already* solved these problems, only we have no conscious access to its contents. Epistemic transcendence is a module-relative notion; mysteries are only mysteries *to* a given faculty. So: do we contain any faculties that are more philosophically gifted than our conscious reason? The way to set about answering this question is to ask whether some other faculty in us *needs* to have the kind of philosophical knowledge or information that reason finds so elusive: what systems would benefit from access to such information? And here two candidates present themselves – the brain and the genes. I shall consider these in turn.

It has become a commonplace to think of the brain as an informational system, ferrying messages along its neural pathways, where the vast majority of these messages have no conscious counterpart. There is every reason to believe that some of these messages relate to the brain's own state, not merely to conditions in the extra-cerebral world, since the brain needs to monitor what is happening at different locations within it. Interhemispheric communication is an obvious example of this kind of intracerebral representation.[16] The physical boundaries of the brain constitute no principled semantic boundary with respect to what the brain is designed to represent. And if the brain is to integrate and coordinate activity within it some implicit theory of its own operations is presumably also implicated – as must also be the case with the other organs of the body whose activity it controls. If the brain is properly to perform its many regulative functions, and if this is to be done informationally, then it makes sense that it should contain some theory of how the entire machine works. Neural signals are not going to be interpretable unless embedded in some story about cerebral and bodily functioning. To put it colourfully, the brain must be a brain scientist, though not of the consciously reasoning variety: it must contain a theory of itself, useful to its functional needs.[17]

But if so, then we must allow for the possibility that it is a *better* brain scientist than those who seek to discover its nature by the use of reason. We must allow, indeed, that it might encode information about its own functioning that *could* not be represented by human reason. Perhaps it employs a level of description of its own workings that has never occurred to us, and never will. And if that were so, then what is an impenetrable mystery for human scientific reason would be no mystery for the brain's own epistemic system. For example, the mystery of how consciousness arises from neural material might be answered by the theory the brain applies to itself in monitoring its state of consciousness. It seems reasonable to suppose that the brain's theory of itself will include psychophysical information as well as information of a purely neural kind, since it needs to effect changes in mental state in appropriate circumstances, e.g. in causing the organism to go to sleep or experience pain. And what goes for consciousness goes for every other mental phenomenon, including those discussed in earlier chapters: all these have a physical basis in the brain, governing their conditions of development and operation, and it would be useful for the brain to represent the principles involved, the better to do its job. When, for example, the brain is called upon to respond to damage to itself, restoring lost or depleted function of a mentalistic kind, it needs the know-how of any architect – some principles by following which the desired result will be achieved. It needs to be an engineer of the mind, capable of generating whatever mental phenomena it subserves.[18] Presumably, then, some grasp (if that is the word) of the nature of the phenomenon has to be involved in this kind of construction. That is to say, if the brain's self-directed causal activity is theory-driven, then it is reasonable to suppose that the theory employed meets certain conditions of optimality – that it is full enough to answer the challenges posed by the tasks the brain has to perform. If one were programming a brain with the information it will need in order to enable it to function as a psychophysical unit, then the sensible strategy would be to build in as much theory as possible. It would make sense, for instance, to incorporate information about the basis of consciousness; ideally, a solution to the mind–body problem would be part of this information.[19] Accordingly, the genetic programme for constructing the human brain might well ensure that the brain's theory of itself is rich enough to solve problems of psychophysical linkage. In consequence, the brain might already incorporate the answers to (at least some) philosophical problems: it is a philosopher of mind as well as a brain scientist, a metaphysician as well as an engineer. It embodies, representationally, the deep principles governing the mental phenomena that so perplex conscious reason.

Nor is the brain constrained as conscious reason is; its representational resources are not governed by the rules that apply to reason. Reason, we said, is serial, slow and sensory (hence spatial); but the brain need not have these characteristics, thus releasing it from whatever theoretical confinement results from them. No doubt it will be subject to its own intrinsic limits, as all epistemic systems must be, but these might be quite at odds with those that constrain reason. Given the brain's particular cognitive slant, it might treat as elementary problems that we find baffling, thus not singling out (say) consciousness and freedom as especially daunting, in comparison with preventing dehydration and hypothermia. If its theory were to be axiomatized, the answers to our philosophical problems might come out as among the simpler theorems to be derived.[20]

Now let us turn to the genetic code, as already anticipated above; and let us follow standard practice in speaking, quite literally, of the information carried by the genes.[21] Then we can inquire into the general properties of this particular epistemic system, comparing them with the properties of reason. Do the instructions encoded in the genes incorporate principles that are beyond the scope of conscious human reason and yet answer to some of reason's perplexities? Well, what are these instructions for, and how successful are the procedures that are guided by them? Plainly, they are instructions for constructing animal bodies, including brains and minds, and the evidence is all around us of how effective these instructions are. The genes certainly know their business: they contain highly detailed specifications for how the resulting organism is to be formed. According to the geneticists, the DNA of a typical human being contains a truly enormous amount of information, enough indeed to specify the blueprint for a human body and its biologically based mental properties. The information storage capacity of the genes is one of their most remarkable characteristics. Also remarkable is the copying capacity of the entire reproductive process; hardly a mistake is made as the information contained in the parents' genes is reproduced in those of the offspring. But these epistemic virtues are purchased at a certain cost – for the genes are virtually ineducable: changes in the environment will not alter the instructions given for constructing the next generation, no matter how disastrous for the organism these instructions may be. Only random mutation can alter the genetic information, reinforced by laborious and lethal natural selection. If reason is the paragon of informational flexibility, then the genes are the epitome of informational rigidity. The course of the organism's experience as it negotiates its environment has no impact on the instructions for building the succeeding generation, while the organism's belief system (if it has one) can keep changing perpetually. Both epistemic systems working together, each with its respective strengths and weaknesses, provide an efficient mechanism for ensuring the survival of the genes (or whatever else you may think to be the unit of natural selection).

The conclusion I am heading towards should now be obvious: given epistemic pluralism, and given some reasonable assumptions about the expressive power of the genes' informational system, we are in a position to take seriously the suggestion that the genes have already solved the philosophical problems mooted earlier – or at least large parts of them. For, first, they must already have solved the problems of purely physical biological engineering, since they contain instructions for building bones and muscles and immune systems and so forth: they represent plans for constructing these organs. But, second, what goes for the body also goes for the mind: in so far as a given mental trait is biologically based, the genes must contain instructions for constructing organisms with that trait. They must, then, represent plans that encode the nature of the trait and the manner of its dependence upon lower-level features of the organism. For example, the human genome must contain specifications for building an organism with conscious states; it must represent plans for producing states there is something it is like to have, and these plans must exploit whatever raw materials the universe actually contains. *We*, of course, have not the slightest idea what these plans might be like – what instructions for manipulating matter they contain – but the genes must know better since they actually perform the task all the time.[22] And similarly for selves, free will, intentionality, knowledge of all kinds: the genes must encode the principles on which the existence of these traits depends (granted that they are genetically programmed, which seems overwhelmingly likely). The genes pass the one true test for theoretical knowledge (or informational power): they can *do* things that depend upon such knowledge (information). Their engineering prowess is evidence of their representational capacity.[23]

Of course, we know very little about how the genes store and use trait-specifying information, and we cannot simply produce a piece of gene lore that explains the possibility of (say) consciousness. But there seems no reason of principle that stands in the way of acknowledging that the genes may well embody a representation of the basic nature of the phenomena we find philosophically puzzling. These phenomena exist, they are biological traits of evolved organisms, and the genes must contain instructions sufficient to generate them: so it is not unreasonable to suppose that the genetic code incorporates the kind of information we seek when we reflect philosophically on those phenomena. If we could but translate that code, rendering it digestible by conscious reason, then we might have the answers we desire: but of course, if TN is right, human reason does not contain the cognitive resources with which to undertake such a translation. Compare language again: the genes must contain a specification of human grammar so that they can generate an innate language faculty with the right properties, but whether a linguist could read grammar off the genetic specifications depends (*inter alia*) on whether his or her reason is capable of representing what the genes already represent – which is by no means a necessary truth.[24] In other words, the solution to the mind–body problem, say, which is written into the genetic code, might be expressed in a language that is not translatable into human language; the properties and principles involved are not graspable by reason, since the genes and human reason have different 'conceptual schemes'.

This conclusion, humbling to reason as it is, ought to reinforce the naturalism inherent in TN. There is, I think, a tendency to suppose that if human intellectual faculties cannot in principle solve a certain kind of problem, then its solution must require supernatural mental faculties, a godlike mind. This prejudice cannot really survive a survey of the cognitive capacities of other species, but its misguidedness is rammed home if it turns out that every cell in your body contains more information about human nature than human reason can ever discover – the genetic blueprint being thus widely distributed. The genes are clearly not miracle minds privy to transnatural information about our constitution; they are brutely natural molecular compounds, and what they encode is similarly earthbound. They just happen to do a job that reason is not called upon to do, where this job requires representational resources that are alien to the purposes of reason. Thus when I say that philosophical questions are mysteries so far as reason is concerned, this should be interpreted against the background of the strong possibility that they are not mysteries so far as the genes are concerned. It is not that we need a supernatural form of conscious reason in order to arrive at the knowledge we seek; rather, we need less conscious reason not more – we need an epistemic system that is free of the constraints proper to reason. The genes, arguably, embody just such a system. They are, in their way, the greatest of geniuses – but a better assessment of the situation is that we need to rethink our concept of a genius.

According to epistemic pluralism, truth is not uniquely the province of reason, but not because some truths are intrinsically unrepresentable. The truths that answer philosophical questions are, according to TN, inaccessible to conscious human reason, but there are, as we have seen, good grounds for supposing that these truths are already represented by other epistemic systems. Conscious states are not necessarily the optimal bearers of all varieties of truth, since they define a specific type of faculty that carries its own inbuilt limits. The assumption that philosophical truth is somehow the proper object of reason – that philosophy and rational thought are inherently made for each other – is what we have been questioning. In fact, rational thought has made very little real progress on the fundamental problems of philosophy, particularly in relation to the nature of our mental attributes; other types of representational system seem better equipped to get at the underlying principles, to judge from their purposes and palpable achievements. The limits of sense or significance cannot therefore be defined in terms of the powers of reason; we need to reckon with the full range of actual and potential representational systems, taking each on its own merits. Theories about the limits of reason (e.g. empiricism) may well have no application to other epistemic systems, especially those that are unconnected to sensory awareness; the concept of observation is not, on this broader view, an indispensable semantic or epistemic concept.[25] TN is a hypothesis specifically about the epistemic powers of the human reasoning faculty, to the effect that this faculty is unsuited to philosophical truth; it does not say that we possess *no* faculty with the requisite epistemic properties. Our brains and our genes may well unconsciously contain the information we consciously seek; unfortunately, this information is so remote from our conscious minds that we cannot derive from it the cognitive satisfaction we crave. The knowledge is in us, but we cannot gain access to it.[26]

NOTES

1 Except that we will not be able to understand the philosophical solutions they patiently (or impatiently!) attempt to explain to us – as they grow blank-eyed when we try to get elementary mechanics across to them.

2 It is surely no accident that geometry was the first area of human thought to achieve rigorous scientific status, as in Euclid: it is as if the relevant module was poised to deliver the goods. The study of mind, however, looks deeply insusceptible to geometrical modes of thought – despite strenuous efforts to construe mental processes in terms of the 'shapes' (n.b.) of mental symbols, as in Fodor, *Psychosemantics*. Geometry is the CALM domain *par excellence*.

3 A point made in several of the contributions to *Consciousness and Contemporary Science*, eds. A. J. Marcel and E. Bisiach.

4 For instance, computer proofs of the four-colour theorem. Fodor stresses the speed differences between perception and cognition in *The Modularity of Mind*; belief formation is slow because it is not an encapsulated reflexive system.

5   As Kant famously said: 'Without sensibility no object would be given to us, without understanding no object would be thought. Thoughts without content are empty, intuitions without concepts are blind.' *Critique of Pure Reason*, p. 93.

6   P. F. Strawson brings out these connections in *Analysis and Metaphysics*. He finds the roots of the most basic feature of thought, namely the distinction between concepts and their instances, in the notion of spatial separation, so that without spatial awareness thought would not be possible for us. Even to think of several instances of the same property requires that we have a general conception of space.

7   The very flexibility of reason carries a large biological risk, since it can bring about major environmental changes without the rest of our biological nature keeping up with these changes. Reason has caused the ozone layer to thin and we might be faced with extinction before we can biologically adapt to the change. Optimally, a biological organ should never cause environmental changes at a faster rate than random mutation and natural selection can keep step with.

8   See Fodor, *The Modularity of Mind*.

9   The language faculty has a specific hard-wired grammar but it is also fully adequate to its cognitive task, and much the same is true of the visual system. But reason, for all its soft-wiring, finds it very difficult to duplicate what these systems achieve so automatically.

10 It is often supposed that the genes selected for something called 'intelligence' and that you get the whole package along with any part of it. But this is insufficiently modular to be plausible, as if a crafty reproducer must also have the capacity for higher learning. Biology goes by the principle that unnecessary baggage should always be minimized. Do we think that monkeys and dolphins have our advanced intellectual capacities in a latent form just because they have propositional attitudes and a complex social life? There is really nothing at all obvious, from a biological point of view, about the human possession of theoretical reason – still less about its supposed omnicompetence. TN says that, on a larger view, our reason actually does have the kind of narrowness of focus that biological principles would lead us to predict, despite its flukish and local excursions into science and culture. And if there were nothing at all we were constitutionally bad at understanding, then we might have to question the biological perspective on human nature that is part of our best theory of the world – and we wouldn't want to have to do that. It is lucky for our theory of ourselves that

there turn out to be theories we cannot grasp. The hardness of philosophy thus confirms human biology.

11 Even in the natural sciences the puzzling areas consist in exceptions to our common sense CALM picture of the spatial world. The trouble with the phenomena I have discussed in earlier chapters is that they lie wholly (or at any rate substantially) beyond this scheme of thought, and are not reachable by modifications in it, so that our puzzlement is comprehensive.

12 The pre-Darwinian idea that we are created by God in his image, though scaled down somewhat, fuels this kind of Rationalist faith, since God's mind is inherently constituted so as to grasp realities of arbitrarily varying kinds. The mind of God is under no naturalistic constraint, because He did not need to evolve; and we partake of this freedom by virtue of our divine origin. But Rationalism of this kind surely crumbles when detached from a religious world-view. We are natural objects all the way down, our minds as much natural products as our bodies; it isn't that we go Godlike from the neck up.

13 For some discussion, see Fred Dretske, *Knowledge and the Flow of Information*. The view is rampant, and rightly so, in the cognitive science literature.

14 See David Marr, *Vision*.

15 We tend to assume that reason is the only (or at least the paradigm) representational system because we have first-person access to its operations; but this is to inflate an epistemic point into an ontological one. To gain a more impartial view of the distribution of semantic properties across the universe it helps to consider how an outside observer might come to assign semantic features to things: such an observer would need to rely upon appropriate theoretical principles to make his attributions, without dependence on the 'givenness' of the semantic – and there is no guarantee that reason would emerge as among the more obvious representational systems that exist. From a detached theoretical point of view, I suspect that the subconscious visual system would be the first to invite semantic description.

16 This kind of communication is highlighted in split-brain cases, in which breakdowns in the normal transfer of information between hemispheres strikingly occur: see M. S. Gazzaniga, *The Bisected Brain*.

17 If we suppose that the brain contains a language in which to carry out its informational transactions, then this language will contain terms that refer to its own states and processes – rather as a computer

employs terms for its own internal states. And it will use these terms to formulate a theory of its own functioning, just as it employs an optical theory in order to interpret the distal significance of an incident pattern of light. Surely, if the brain can subserve the representational powers of our conscious reason, then it also has the resources with which to subserve extensive tracts of representation that do *not* show up in our conscious beliefs. My speculative guess is that the brain employs only a small fraction of its representational machinery in the maintenance of our conscious beliefs; the rest is devoted to performing tasks of which we have, and need, no awareness. Among these tasks, I am suggesting, are some that rely upon representations of the brain's own deep principles of functioning, including those that relate to mental phenomena.

18   Let me be clear that I am not saying merely that the brain needs to contain the engineering machinery essential to the mental phenomena it generates – that is a truism. I am saying that it needs to contain a *theory* of this machinery – a symbolic representation of the relevant science and technology. It is both machine and machine superviser.

19   Thus it would contain a suitable representation of the property *P* discussed in my *The Problem of Consciousness* – that property which links consciousness intelligibly to the brain but whose identity is closed to conscious reason.

20   A clarification may be in order here. My point is not that whenever the brain gives rise to a mental phenomenon it does so by exploiting semantic properties, so that (say) the predicate 'pain' always occurs in the causal genesis of sensations of pain. Rather, the brain contains a self-monitoring subsystem which keeps semantic track of its current state, so that appropriate changes can be initiated when necessary. For example, it might incorporate a unit that instructs the pain centres to shift fibres when neurological fatigue has rendered the current fibres unable to carry on subserving a sensation of pain. Semantically mediated feedback loops would clearly be very useful for self-regulatory purposes, and the cleverer they are the better. Then the point in the text is that the dimensions of this cleverness might lie athwart those available to reason.

21   Richard Dawkins gives a pleasingly literal account of this in *The Blind Watchmaker*, chapter 5.

22   I use 'know' here in a sense that does not require consciousness and belief – merely effective representation. I suspect, in fact, that that is pretty much what the word means in ordinary language, but nothing I say depends upon this.

23 A question can be raised as to level of description employed by the genes in constructing organs of the body and mind: should we say that the genes represent only microproperties of organs, such as the protein compounds that are assembled during ontogenesis, or can we also say that they represent macroproperties of such organs, as (say) that of being a heart or a kidney or a pain sensation? In other words, does the genetic code refer only to the biochemical supervenience basis of organs or does it describe matters in terms proper to what supervenes? For, plainly, the job will get done under either assumption, since supervenience guarantees that the requisite organs will duly come into existence. This is a fairly complex question, but I would note the following points in favour of the more generous alternative. First, we could raise the same question about any kind of informationally driven engineer, human or animal: does the bird or the beaver or the construction worker represent what they build as a *nest* or a *dam* or a *house*? I would say yes, but it is also true in these cases that the same task could be performed by representing only the constituents of these things and their relations. Second, semantic content is tied to function, and it is the function of bits of genetic material to produce organs of various macro-types: the particular genes in question exist *because* they produce hearts and kidneys and consciousness – these natural kinds being what natural selection selects for. Third, and related, organs can be grouped together according to their macro-functions despite there being multiple physical realizations of the function in question; and hence the genes that code for these organs need themselves to be grouped together, semantically, at this higher level of description, on pain of missing biological generalizations. Fourth, it seems to me intuitively obvious – as well as theoretically useful – to characterize genetic instructions as pertaining to higher levels than that of protein constituents: why resist the convenience this kind of ascription of content affords? Once we have gone epistemically pluralist it seems pointless to insist that the genes can only speak the language of proteins and are not able to express other biological properties.

24 This presupposes the position defended in the previous footnote, namely that the genetic specifications advert to properties of what gets produced and not merely to properties of what goes into producing it. Theoretically, grammar could be innately specified simply by programming for biochemical structures that are *sufficient* to secure grammatical representations – without actually specifying grammatical properties themselves. So grammar could in principle be genetically encoded only *de re* not *de dicto*. However, I think

it is more natural, once grammar has been agreed to be genetically determined, to take the genes to contain information *de dicto* about grammatical features, especially once it is recognized that the *same* grammatical properties could be variously realized, physically, in different organisms. So if there is an innate module representing the structure of human languages, as there plausibly is, then there is also a specification of this structure (*de dicto*) in the genetic code: the genes already know (or encode) what the rational linguist is struggling to discover.

25 Compare Fodor, 'The Dogma that Didn't Bark (A Fragment of a Naturalized Epistemology)'. Fodor argues, correctly I think, that scientific theory construction does not necessarily involve the making of perceptual observations: this is just one method of belief fixation. I am making the same kind of point about epistemic systems that proceed without benefit of reason and belief: we need an epistemology that generalizes across different epistemic systems and does not treat human reason, aided by observation, as *definitive* of theory construction and epistemic warrant.

26 We might be reminded here of the Freudian unconscious, which is also said to contain contentful states to which conscious reason has little or no access. In principle, according to Freudian theory, the unconscious might harbour concepts to which the conscious mind is cognitively closed, if repression were sufficiently effective; and these concepts might feature in theories that are needed to explain phenomena to which we do have conscious access. This, then, would be a case in which TN holds with respect to conscious reason but not with respect to the conceptual resources of the unconscious. The case is analogous to that of the frustrated linguist and his subconscious language faculty. What I am saying about philosophy, reason and the genetic code belongs in the same class of possibility claims.

9

The Future of Philosophy

Different metaphilosophies are associated with distinct conceptions of the nature of philosophical difficulty, and hence with varying views about what philosophical progress would consist in, if we could make any. Positivism held that philosophical questions were strictly meaningless unless analytically or empirically decidable, so that the recalcitrance of traditional metaphysical questions was symptomatic of their emptiness or nonfactuality. Progress would consist in recognizing this, ceasing to ask the questions, and pursuing other less ambitious aims.[1] The later Wittgenstein (and those of like mind) took philosophical difficulty to result from intellectual confusions generated by the forms of our language and by the temptation to assimilate disparate concepts.[2] For him, progress would have to come from dispelling these confusions by means of a perspicuous representation of our concepts; though whether he thought we could be fully and finally released from these confusions, so that our philosophical perplexities vanish, is perhaps not clear. Certain analytic philosophers (in one sense of the term) take it that the difficulty of philosophical questions results from the deep implicitness of their answers in our given conceptual scheme; the requisite knowledge lies so buried in our thought and language, so far from the surface they present, that we find it excruciatingly hard to excavate it.[3] Progress would accordingly consist in penetrating more deeply, by means of 'analysis', into the underlying content or structure of the ordinary concepts we bring to bear. What might be described as the traditional or lay conception of philosophical difficulty locates it directly in the special subject-matter of the questions: we are inquiring into intrinsically profound or subtle or intricate matters, ontologically set apart from the mundane world of science. This conception is probably not separable, at least historically, from religious tenets: philosophy is concerned, supremely among human studies, with subjects bordering on the divine – with questions in whose answers God is likely to figure. Progress, if possible at all, would have to come from enhanced insight into this super-natural order, using whatever means might be vouchsafed to mere mortals. Transcendental naturalism, the view defended here, accounts for the difficulty of philosophy in terms of inherent structural limitations on the human intellect: reason is not con-structed so as to be sensitive to philosophical truth. Progress would require us to overcome these architectural or constitutive limitations – which is not going to be possible without entirely reshaping the human mind. The reason we find philosophical knowledge so hard to obtain, according to TN, is not that we are asking vacuous pseudo-questions, nor that we are bewitched away from commanding a clear view of our own ordinary concepts, nor that the truth lies concealed too deeply within our conceptual scheme, nor that we are dealing with a peculiarly rarified ontology. It is, rather, that we are trying to force our cognitive faculties to deliver knowledge of phenomena whose nature those faculties are not cut out to comprehend. The questions are real enough, we are not notably confused about the concepts involved, we are not blind to the correct analysis of those concepts, the phenomena themselves are not intrinsically other-worldly; our problem is simply that we lack the necessary mental organs with which to form theories of the phenomena that puzzle us. The explanation of the hardness of philosophy is thus of the same general category as the explanation for why a blind person cannot form concepts for colours, or why human beings cannot fly, or why dogs have no musical appreciation – lacks for which the other kinds of explanation cited would presumably be absurd.[4] TN, we might say, takes our philosophical incapacity at face value.

It is important to recognize, what should be obvious, that these different views of the nature of philosophical difficulty are genuine rivals, competing hypotheses about the source of an acknowledged cognitive lack. They represent divergent historical trends that have arisen in response to an accepted (and lamentable) fact. There is something special, they all agree, about philosophical ignorance, as contrasted with ignorance of other kinds, both as to its quality and its persistence, and so a distinctive story is required to account for it. The absence of progress that is so markedly characteristic of philosophy must be represented as having a special source, of a peculiarly obstructive kind. The hypothesis I have been advancing, which offers its own particular kind of explanation of what holds us back, also has its historical roots: elements of it can be found, sometimes quite strikingly, in Locke and Hume, in Kant and Schopenhauer, and most recently in Chomsky.[5] The essence of the position, as I am construing it here, consists principally in a firm separation of ontology and epistemology, and an unswervingly naturalistic view of human cognitive capacity. From the perspective of TN, the history of speculative thought, with its areas of advancement and retardation, is a reflection of the biases built into our cognitive systems, of their specific design-features and modes of operation. Cognitive phylogeny recapitulates cognitive modularity. Other beings, differently constituted, might trace an inverted intellectual history, with philosophy among the earlier triumphs of their intellectual endeavours and physics lagging embarrassingly behind.

Clearly, TN is a large-scale high-altitude hypothesis about the human mind. No crucial experiment could establish or refute it, and any evidence we might produce is bound to be inconclusive and variously interpretable. In this respect it resembles other hypotheses of comparable scale and generality – say, the global warming hypothesis. We must go by general trends, tentative suggestions as to mechanism, a sense of relative plausibility. That such grand hypotheses are necessarily highly conjectural and indirectly supported is no reason not to take them seriously; due caution must of course be exercised in assenting to them, but we can reasonably hope to assess their relative probability and explanatory strength. TN asks for no more than that: not firm conviction but considered estimation. It asks to be treated like any other empirical hypothesis of comparable status.

It might now help, in gaining the right perspective on TN, to consider the following question: what would be the most plausible hypothesis to adopt about the nature of philosophical difficulty if, in a million years time, the subject were in much the same state it is in now? Suppose, that is, that the DIME shape still characterizes the field, with philosophers lining up in roughly the same proportions as today: there are the same disputes, the same uncertainties, the same wavering, the same dogmatizing. Suppose, too, that other intellectual disciplines have reached a steady state, boasting general consensus, a fixed body of knowledge, an atmosphere of intellectual serenity. Then I venture to suggest that TN will at that time seem like the obvious and natural position to adopt. Human beings will have done all the conceptual analysis they are ever likely to do, and their sciences will have been brought to their peak (minus any stubbornly 'philosophical' remnants); so those two hopes for the resolution of philosophical problems will have been long since abandoned. It will then, I predict, seem eminently reasonable to believe that the human mind is simply not suited to answering the kinds of question philosophers raise.

And now let me boldly speculate that this *will* be the state of philosophy in a million years time, give or take some streamlining and clarification: the fundamental disputes will still rage, as irresoluble as ever, as they have these many centuries. But if that prediction is plausible, then the right conclusion to draw *now* is that TN is the most reasonable position to adopt: it is just that we have not had as long to read the writing on the wall, plainly inscribed though it is. In other words, if we consider candidly what the long-term prospects for philosophical inquiry are, then it begins to seem that something like TN *has* to be true – since deep-seated perplexity appears endemic to the field. Surely we shall never, in respect of the questions I discussed in earlier chapters, arrive at the kind of intellectual stasis and solidity that typifies so much of the natural sciences. Philosophical questions look essentially contentious, chronically debatable. There is certainly no sense in the air that we are heading for any basic convergence of opinion. We cannot even so much as agree on whether the things we are interested in really *exist*. The future of philosophy will be, I surmise, much like its past and present; and TN has a theory for why this should be so.[6]

It remains to broach some practical questions about TN and the activity of philosophizing. What should would-be philosophers *do* granted that TN is the correct position? What value, if any, can philosophy have under that supposition? How depressed should we feel about the truth of TN?

As to the first question, there is no avoiding the obvious answer: there is nothing much they *can* do. That is, if the class of problems I have discussed is really undecidable in principle by the human intellect, then there is no point in trying to solve these problems – you might as well try to leap unaided to the moon. Since this kind of knowledge is literally unobtainable, it is pointless to strive to obtain it, if the point of an activity is to be judged by its prospects of success. We must simply acquiesce in our constitutional limitations. Two qualifying observations can be made, however. First, TN is not *certainly* correct, so that, decision-theoretically, it is rational to continue to act on the assumption that it *might* be false, in the hope that it may be: for it would be bad to foreclose the possibility of philosophical knowledge when there is even a chance that it is achievable. And, second, much of what is done under the name 'philosophy' can still be done even granted the truth of TN: conceptual analysis, the systematization of the sciences, ethics and politics, and no doubt other things. An interesting question to consider here, itself philosophical, is how much of what is traditionally classified as philosophy is actually subject to TN, given that part of it is. So it is not as if, in acknowledging that a certain class of questions is unsolvable, philosophers will have nothing left to do with their skills and time.

As to the second question, what the value of philosophy might be granted TN, we must again return the obvious answer: concerning the unresolvable component at least, its value cannot consist in the acquisition of knowledge, since the requisite knowledge is just not acquirable.[7] There can, indeed, still be value in thinking through the alternatives, assessing their import and relative plausibility – and value too in appreciating where one's powers of comprehension falter. But the value of philosophy cannot consist in the production of the kind of positive theoretical knowledge of the world that the sciences offer; it cannot supply that sort of intellectual satisfaction. Its value must rather lie in the humility encouraged by recognizing our limitations. And there is the consolation that we can obtain knowledge *that* we are subject to limitations on what we can know: knowledge of our incurable ignorance is, after all, one kind of knowledge, and quite an interesting kind at that.

Third, we must ask how regrettable the truth of TN is. It is certainly disappointing to arrive at the view that the questions that most engage one's interest are not soluble – that does rather take the wind out of one's sails. But the depression this is apt to induce might be mitigated by the following considerations. First, from the perspective of TN, philosophical knowledge would not have the kind of objective profundity we tend to project onto the subject; for this is largely an artifact of our cognitive limits, not an accurate measure of where the correct theory would stand in some objective ranking. As we have noted before, those talented Martians who naturally possess the solutions to our problems might regard the knowledge they have as intrinsically rather trivial and shallow; if we could but share it we might suffer a disappointingly deflationary sense of bathos. Secondly, it might be that we are so constituted that, in order to have the philosophical knowledge we desire, we would have to be totally different sorts of psychological being: we might have to sacrifice all that is distinctive in human nature, our very mode of sensibility, in order to possess the kinds of faculties that would smoothly deliver philosophical knowledge.[8] And this might be a type of being we would prefer, on balance, not to be. Given such cognitive exclusivity, philosophical aptitude might be a trait we would rather do without. If Satan came to offer us the trade, we would be wise to hesitate before accepting the necessary alterations to our nature.[9]

NOTES

1   See A. J. Ayer, *Language, Truth and Logic*.
2   Wittgenstein, *Philosophical Investigations*, especially sections 90–133.
3   Thus P. F. Strawson, *Analysis and Metaphysics*. He likens the task of the philosopher to that of the linguist striving to articulate the deep structure of our language – both try to make explicit what is already known implicitly.
4   We can surely *imagine* a species of thinking creatures whose inability to answer a certain range of questions has the TN kind of explanation – as we can imagine other creatures whose perplexities are

to be explained along the lines of the other metaphilosophies mentioned. The question, then, is which of these conceivable explanations of our philosophical difficulties is actually true of us; and TN offers itself as the most plausible theory in the field. It helps, in deciding the question, to imagine a species for which TN is true by stipulation and then comparing this species to our own. Philosophical activity would, I think, look suggestively similar in the two cases, thus inviting an inference to a common explanation.

5 Schopenhauer, in particular, favours a biologically naturalistic picture of our cognitive limits, recasting Kant in these terms. He compares the bounds of the human intellect to the restricted receptivities of a plant to external influences, observing that this 'picture can thus make it comprehensible to us why the realm of the human intellect should have such narrow boundaries, as Kant demonstrates it has in the *Critique of Pure Reason*' (*Essays and Aphorisms*, p. 122). The human intellect, for Schopenhauer, exists to serve the will, so that it is 'a quite abnormal event if in some man intellect deserts its natural vocation . . . in order to occupy itself purely objectively. But it is precisely this which is the origin of art, poetry and philosophy, which are therefore not produced by an organ intended for that purpose' (p. 127). For Schopenhauer, the profundity of the problems of philosophy has no objective correlate: the depth of the problems arises merely from the biologically determined structures of our intellect.

6 I take wry pleasure in the thought that TN will probably be the orthodox opinion in the dying stages of the sun's heat . . .

7 Russell, in 'The Value of Philosophy', remarks that 'there are many questions – and among them those that are of the profoundest interest to our spiritual life – which, so far as we can see, must remain insoluble to the human intellect unless its powers become of a quite different order from what they are now.' This leads him to conclude that the value of philosophy cannot consist in the establishing of a body of known truths; instead, he says, it must lie in the very uncertainty that is characteristic of philosophical reflection. See *The Problems of Philosophy*, p. 155 and chapter XV.

8 Compare Chomsky, *Language and Problems of Knowledge*: 'We suppose that humans are part of the natural world. They plainly have the capacity to solve certain problems. It follows that they lack the capacity to solve other problems, which will either be far too difficult for them to handle within existing limitations of time, memory, and so on or will literally be beyond the scope of their intelligence in principle. The human mind cannot be in Descartes's terms a "universal instrument which can serve for all contingencies".

That is fortunate, for if it were such a universal instrument, it would serve equally badly for all contingencies. We could deal with no problems at all with any measure of success' (p. 149). And again: 'A creature is fortunate if there are problems that it cannot solve, because this means that it has the capacity to solve certain other problems well' (p. 148).

9   It is by no means inconceivable that the special character of our art and our personal relationships depends upon the cognitive biases and limits that prevent us handling philosophical problems, so that philosophical aptitude would deprive our lives of much of their point. Philosophy might require even more self-sacrifice than has traditionally been conceded.

References

Ayer, A. J., *Language, Truth and Logic*. New York: Dover, 1952.

Benacerraf, P., 'Mathematical Truth', *Journal of Philosophy*, 70 (1973): 661–80.

Berkeley, G., *A Treatise Concerning the Principles of Human Knowledge*, in D. Armstrong, ed., *Berkeley's Philosophical Writings*. New York: Macmillan, 1965.

Block, N., ed., *Readings in the Philosophy of Psychology*. Cambridge, MA: Harvard University Press, 1981.

Block, N., 'Troubles with Functionalism', in Block, ed., 1981.

Chomsky, N., *Reflections on Language*. UK: Fontana, 1976.

Chomsky, N., *Rules and Representations*. New York: Columbia University Press, 1980.

Chomsky, N., *Language and Problems of Knowledge*. Cambridge, MA: MIT Press, 1988.

Churchland, P., 'Eliminative Materialism and Propositional Attitudes', *The Journal of Philosophy*, 78, no. 2 (1981): 67–89.

Davidson, D., 'Mental Events', in D. Davidson, *Essays on Actions and Events*. Oxford: Clarendon Press, 1980: 207–25.

Davidson, D., 'Freedom to Act', in Davidson, 1980.

Davidson, D., 'Agency', in Davidson, 1980.

Davidson, D., 'A Coherence Theory of Truth and Knowledge', in D. Henrich, *Kant oder Hegel*. Klett-Cotta: 1983.

Davidson, D., *Inquiries into Truth and Interpretation*. Oxford: Clarendon Press, 1984.

Dawkins, R., *The Blind Watchmaker*. Harlow: Longman Scientific and Technical, 1986.

Dennett, D., *The Intentional Stance*. Cambridge, MA: MIT Press, 1989.

Descartes, R., *Meditations on First Philosophy*, trans. J. Cottingham. Cambridge: Cambridge University Press, 1986.

Dretske, F., *Knowledge and the Flow of Information*. Cambridge, MA: MIT Press, 1981.

Dummett, M., 'What is a Theory of Meaning?', in S. Guttenplan, ed., *Mind and Language: Wolfson College Lectures 1974*. Oxford: Clarendon Press, 1975.

Eccles, J. and K. Popper, *The Self and Its Brain*. Berlin: Springer–Verlag, 1977.

Evans, G., *The Varieties of Reference*. Oxford: Clarendon Press, 1982.

Farrell, B., 'Experience', *Mind*, 59 (1950): 170–98.

Field, H., *Science without Numbers*. Princeton: Princeton University Press, 1980.

Fodor, J. A., *The Modularity of Mind: An Essay on Faculty Psychology*. Cambridge, MA: MIT Press, 1983.

Fodor, J. A., *Psychosemantics*. Cambridge, MA: MIT Press, 1987.

Fodor, J. A., *A Theory of Content and Other Essays*. Cambridge, MA: MIT Press, 1990.

Fodor, J. A., 'The Dogma that Didn't Bark (A Fragment of Naturalized Epistemology)', *Mind*, 100 (2), April, 1991: 201–20.

Gazzaniga, M., *The Bisected Brain*. New York: Appleton–Century–Crofts, 1970.

Gödel, K., 'What is Cantor's Continuum Problem?', in P. Benacerraf and H. Putnam, eds, *Philosophy of Mathematics: Selected Readings*, second edition. Cambridge: Cambridge University Press, 1983.

Goodman, N., *Fact, Fiction and Forecast*. Cambridge, MA: Harvard University Press, 1983.

Honderich, T., *Essays on Freedom of Action*. London: Routledge and Kegan Paul, 1973

Hume, D., *A Treatise of Human Nature*. Oxford: Clarendon Press, 1978.

Hume, D., *An Enquiry Concerning Human Understanding*, ed. L. A. Selby-Bigge. Oxford: Clarendon Press, 1982.

James, W., *Principles of Psychology*, vols I and II. New York: Holt, 1890.

Kant, I., *Critique of Pure Reason*, trans. N. Kemp Smith. London: Macmillan, 1929.

Kim, J., 'Psychophysical Supervenience', *Philosophical Studies* 41, 1982.

Kripke, S., *Naming and Necessity*. Cambridge, MA: Harvard University Press, 1980.

Kripke, S., *Wittgenstein on Rules and Private Language*. Cambridge, MA: Harvard University Press, 1982.

Marcel, A. J. and E. Bisiach, *Consciousness in Contemporary Science*. Oxford: Clarendon Press, 1988.

Marr, D., *Vision*. San Francisco: W. H. Freeman, 1982.

McClelland, J. L. and D. E. Rumelhart, *Parallel Distributed Processing: Explorations in the Microstructure of Cognition*. Cambridge, MA: MIT Press, 1986.

McGinn, C., 'A priori and A posteriori Knowledge', *Proceedings of the Aristotelian Society*, March, 1976.

McGinn, C., 'Philosophical Materialism', *Synthese*, June, 1980.

McGinn, C., *The Character of Mind*. Oxford: Oxford University Press, 1982.

McGinn, C., *The Subjective View*. Oxford: Oxford University Press, 1982.

McGinn, C., *Wittgenstein on Meaning*. Oxford: Blackwell, 1984.

McGinn, C., *Mental Content*. Oxford: Blackwell, 1989.

McGinn, C., 'The Hidden Structure of Consciousness', in C. McGinn, *The Problem of Consciousness*. Oxford: Blackwell, 1991.

Millikan, R., *Language, Thought, and Other Biological Categories*. Cambridge, MA: MIT Press, 1984.

Moore, G., 'Proof of an External World', in G. E. Moore, *Philosophical Papers*. London: 1959.

Nagel, T., 'What Is It Like To Be A Bat?', in T. Nagel, *Mortal Questions*. Cambridge: Cambridge University Press, 1979.

Nagel, T., *The View From Nowhere*. Oxford: Oxford University Press, 1986.

Nozick, R., *Philosophical Explanations*. Oxford: Oxford University Press, 1981.

Parfit, D., *Reasons and Persons*. Oxford: Oxford University Press, 1984.

Perry, J., *Personal Identity*. Berkeley: University of California Press, 1975.

Plato, *The Republic*, in E. Hamilton and H. Cairns, eds, *Plato: The Collected Dialogues*. Princeton: Princeton University Press, 1961.

Putnam, H., *Reason, Truth and History*. Cambridge: Cambridge University Press, 1981.

Quine, W. V. O., *Word and Object*. Cambridge, MA: MIT Press, 1960.

Quine, W. V. O., 'Two Dogmas of Empiricism', in W. V. O. Quine, *From a Logical Point of View*. Cambridge, MA: Harvard University Press, 1980.

Rosenthal, D., 'Two Concepts of Consciousness', in D. Rosenthal, ed., *The Nature of Mind*. Oxford: Oxford University Press, 1991.

Russell, B., *The Problems of Philosophy*. Oxford: Oxford University Press, 1919.

Russell, B., *Logic and Knowledge*. London: Unwin and Hyman, 1956.

Sartre, J.-P., *The Transcendence of the Ego*, trans. F. Williams and R. Kirkpatrick. New York: Noonday Press, 1957.

Sartre, J.-P., *Being and Nothingness*. New York: Washington Square Press, 1966.

Schopenhauer, A., *Essays and Aphorisms*. London: Penguin, 1970.

Searle, J., *The Rediscovery of the Mind*. Cambridge, MA: MIT Press, 1992.

Sellars, W., 'Empiricism and the Philosophy of Mind', in *Minnesota Studies in the Philosophy of Science, Vol I*. Minneapolis: University of Minnesota Press, 1956: 253–329.

Stich, S., *From Folk Psychology to Cognitive Science: The Case Against Belief*. Cambridge, MA: MIT Press, 1983.

Strawson, G., *Freedom and Belief*. Oxford: Oxford University Press, 1986.

Strawson, P., *Individuals*. London: Methuen, 1959.

Strawson, P., 'Freedom and Resentment', in P. Strawson, *Freedom and Resentment*. London: Methuen, 1974.

Strawson, P., *Analysis and Metaphysics: An Introduction to Philosophy*. Oxford: Oxford University Press, 1992.

Stroud, B., *The Significance of Philosophical Scepticism*. Oxford: Oxford University Press, 1984.

Unger, P., *Ignorance: A Case for Scepticism*. Oxford: Oxford University Press, 1975.

Williams, B., *Problems of the Self*. Cambridge: Cambridge University Press, 1973.

Wittgenstein, L., *The Blue and Brown Books*. Oxford: Blackwell, 1960.

Wittgenstein, L., *Tractatus Logico-Philosophicus*. London: Routledge and Kegan Paul, 1961.

Wittgenstein, L., *On Certainty*. Oxford: Blackwell, 1969.

Wittgenstein, L., *Philosophical Investigations*. Oxford: Blackwell, 1974.

Wittgenstein, L., *Zettel*. Oxford: Blackwell, 1981.

Index